10⁰⁰

PRAYING
FOR YOUR
UNBORN CHILD

FRANCIS MacNUTT
and
JUDITH MacNUTT

Drawings by René Graef

Complete and Unabridged

AN IMAGE BOOK
DOUBLEDAY
NEW YORK   LONDON   TORONTO   SYDNEY   AUCKLAND

AN IMAGE BOOK
PUBLISHED BY DOUBLEDAY
a division of Bantam Doubleday Dell Publishing Group, Inc.
1540 Broadway, New York, New York 10036

IMAGE, DOUBLEDAY, and the portrayal of a deer drinking
from a stream are trademarks of Doubleday, a division
of Bantam Doubleday Dell Publishing Group, Inc.

Image Books Edition published October 1989
by special arrangement with Doubleday.

The authors wish to thank the following for permission to quote from
previously published materials:

Bridge Publishing Co. for excerpts from *Feeling and Healing Your Emotions*
by Dr. Conrad Baars, copyright © 1979 by Conrad Baars. Reprinted by
permission of the publisher.

Darton, Longman & Todd, Ltd., for excerpts from *Tight Corners in Pastoral
Counseling* by Frank Lake, copyright © 1981 by Frank Lake. Reprinted by
permission of the publisher.

Fleming H. Revell Co. for excerpts from *Will I Cry Tomorrow?* by Dr. Susan
Stanford, copyright © 1987 by Susan Stanford. Reprinted by permission of the
publisher.

Summit Books for excerpts from *The Secret Life of the Unborn Child* by
Thomas Verny, M.D., with John Kelly, copyright © 1981 by Thomas Verny,
M.D., and John Kelly. Reprinted by permission of the publisher.

Library of Congress Cataloging-in-Publication Data
MacNutt, Francis.
  Praying for your unborn child
  Francis MacNutt and Judith MacNutt; drawings by René Graef.
    p. cm.
  "An Image book."
  "Complete and unabridged."
  Includes bibliographical references.
  ISBN 0-385-23282-9
  1. Parents—Religious life. 2. Prayer—
Christianity. 3. Pregnant women—
Religious life. 4. Fetus—Religious
aspects—Christianity. I. MacNutt, Judith. II. Title.
[BV4529.M33 1989]
248.8′4—dc19   88-35924
               CIP

12 11 10 9 8 7 6 5

CONTENTS

DEDICATED
WITH LOVE
TO
RACHEL
("LAMB OF GOD")
AND
DAVID
("BELOVED OF GOD")

and all the other beautiful children
who have been an inspiration
to us
and taught us so much of
what we share in this book

PREFACE

We need to mention just a few things about our book.

For one thing, we had a hard time coming to a decision about whether to refer to the unborn child (since, without a sonogram, we can't determine its sex) as "it," "he," or "she." "It" sounds too impersonal for a human being; yet, if we use "he" or "she" throughout, someone might accuse us of sexism. So we chose a simple solution: in all the chapters that Francis wrote, the unborn child is "he"; in the chapters that Judith wrote, the child is "she."

We used several translations of the Bible, sometimes choosing one translation over another because it made a particular point in a more forceful way. A rule of thumb is that (unless otherwise marked) Judith uses the Revised Standard Version (RSV) in her chapters and Francis uses the Jerusalem Bible (JB) in his. At times, we also use the New Jerusalem Bible (NJB) and the New International Version (NIV).

We want, in a very special way, to thank everyone who helped in writing the book. In particular, we thank those whose letters we use in our text; to protect their identity, we have changed their names (for the most part), although their letters are quoted accurately. Then, we especially thank our secretary, Mrs. Bobbi O'Malley, who has spent hours of her spare time typing the manuscript and transferring it to her husband's word processor. We thank our obstetrician, too, Dr. Sally Osborne, who took time in her busy schedule to give us an afternoon's interview to share a doctor's perspective on praying for mothers and their unborn children. It was Sally who—only two days before giving birth to her own son—helped bring our son, David, into this world.

Francis and Judith MacNutt

January 22, 1987

PRAYING
FOR YOUR
UNBORN CHILD

INTRODUCTION
TO YOU, OUR READER

(by Francis)

For the past four years, we have eagerly desired to write this book. We are excited by what might happen when pregnant mothers and expectant fathers learn to pray for their baby, who is waiting to be born. We believe that, if enough parents start praying for their unborn children, a gentle revolution will take place. The babies to be born will become a new, different generation—more disposed to love God, happier and more secure.

Just as the unborn John the Baptist "leapt for joy" in Elizabeth's womb, when Mary's greeting reached her ears, so your little child can respond to you—and to God—when you pray. This can make a real difference in your child's health—physical and emotional—as we hope to show; but, even more important, your child will be blessed and filled with the life of God, to the limit of his infant capacity, from the moment his little life begins.

Similarly, the Word of God came to Jeremiah:

> "Before I formed you in the womb I knew you; before you came to birth I consecrated you; I appointed you as a prophet to the nations" (*Jr.* 1:5, NJB).

While your child may not be called to be a prophet, Jesus really wants to consecrate your child, to fill him with love and bring him into his Father's family. We want to share with you some of the wondrous ways in which this can happen to your own child.

We have had the moving experience of praying with our own children—Rachel (now five years old) and David (now three)—and know that the beauty and power of prayer, far from being some vague ideal, is very real. When Rachel was two years old, our pediatrician told us that the average child her age falls sick eight times a year; that year she was only sick twice (simply with colds). I'm sure that other factors are involved, but we still believe that the most important factor in her health is the protective power of Jesus for which we pray every day.

We want to share the good news—the GOOD NEWS—that praying together for your children can make a great difference.

The sad thing is that so few Christian parents seem to realize how much they can help their children (and themselves) by praying for the unborn child. This lack of prayer only reflects the larger picture that Christian parents seldom pray *with* their children at any time in their lives.

In *The Prayer that Heals,*[1] I mention that only about 3 percent of the nearly hundred thousand people I had asked (in audiences that I was addressing on the topic of praying in the family) could remember their *fathers* ever praying *with* them *in his own words.* And only about 20 percent could remember their *mothers* ever praying with them. In the six years since I wrote that book those percentages still hold true.

But the results are still more pitiful when I ask parents how many of them have *ever prayed together* for their *unborn* children still being carried in the mother's womb. Praying for the unborn child—husband and wife together—is such a natural thing to do that we might expect that most Christian parents would do it. (Especially since I know of no church or pastor who would object to such a beautiful practice.) Yet, we have questioned more than ten thousand parents, and only about 1 percent in a typical Sunday congregation seem ever to have prayed together for their unborn children!

We are convinced that extraordinary changes in the health and happiness of children will take place if you really believe that Jesus—that prayer—can make a real difference. Psychiatrists, such as Dr. Thomas Verny,[2] are saying that the unborn child picks up on his parents' feelings and thoughts in an extraordinary way and that the *greatest help or detriment* in determining the child's emotional and physical health is the *mother's attitude* toward the fetus. This unborn child is not just a physical body, but is already sensing whether he is loved or rejected. Crucial, too, is the father's relationship toward his unborn child; he provides the mother with the love and security of a strong relationship and that security in some mysterious way is passed on to that little child, waiting in darkness to be born.

What more beautiful way of turning the love of mother and father toward that child than when they are praying together!

Yet, we hope this book helps more than expectant parents. Within each one of us there is a little child that went through this whole birthing process—perhaps even as long as seventy years ago. If there is anything that was wounded—physically or psychologically—in your birth, it may still be affecting you today by weighing you down with some mysterious fear or anxiety. As Dr. Verny states:

". . . The womb is the child's first world. How he experiences it—as friendly or hostile—does create personality and character *predispositions.* The womb, in a very real sense, establishes the child's expectations. If it has been a warm, loving environment, the child is likely to expect the outside world to be the same. This produces a predisposition toward trust, openness, extroversion and self-confidence. The world will be his oyster, just as the womb has been. If that environment has been hostile, the child will anticipate that his new world will be equally uninviting. He will be predisposed toward suspiciousness, distrust and introversion. Relating to others will be hard, and so will self-assertion. Life will be more difficult for him than for a child who had a good womb experience."[3]

Perhaps you will recognize as you read this book that there was something wounded or missing in your early life. The good news, though, is that, no matter how early that wound occurred, Jesus can heal that fear (or fill that emptiness) and set you free.

For instance, we conducted a workshop on inner healing at Aldersgate 1982 (the annual conference of the National United Methodist Charismatic Fellowship) in Des Moines, Iowa. We decided to concentrate on the area of praying for the unborn child. Perhaps six hundred people came to our workshop and when we told them what our topic would be, some thought, "What am I doing here? I don't need to learn about praying for the unborn: my children are all grown." Yet, they told us afterward that they found the workshop was specially meant for them; in the healing prayer we made at the workshop's end, many of them experienced a healing of their own inner child that they never dreamed possible.

Several times Judith and I have discovered separately, in praying with people for inner healing, that, occasionally, the person would suddenly begin reexperiencing his birth, saying, "I'm not going to be born! I'm not going to come out!" Then we had to pray to heal the trauma of birth. This has happened now a number of times, to both of us. Such dramatic experiences have helped us realize how much that very earliest time of our life may need healing. Several times the person we were praying for actually fell to the ground and curled up in a fetal position. Some of these extraordinary manifestations have happened while we were praying in silence, and the power of suggestion cannot account for the sudden return to the earliest stage of life. It is as if their wounds were just waiting to surface when the power of the Spirit was present to heal. But those wounds are so painful and so deep that they may never heal until the love of Jesus is present to make it bearable to face them again. And not just face them; Jesus will heal them.

As one young man wrote, after such an experience:

"You asked how I felt during the few minutes you laid hands on me the night before, October 12, 1985. My heart felt melted and pliable for about the sixth time in my life (I am thirty-one). It was as if Jesus massaged my heart, and turned it over and over in his hands, to make something beautiful for God from the clay that was once stone. I can't explain what happened when I rested in the fetal position, but I know I rested in the Spirit, and breathed heavily.

"Later I felt as if nothing mattered as I walked out of the meeting room to have some food with friends. I had met God and he was everything. He loved me and he healed me.

"I also believe that this healing cannot be duplicated by secular science. I should know: I spent four years in psychoanalysis after I had an emotional breakdown at age thirteen.

"I feel as if I can finally pray 'Abba,' and I definitely know the posture of a young child before his daddy. Perhaps this prenatal healing has freed me to communicate with God the Father where, before, I could only communicate with Jesus. I praise God for that freedom!"

How encouraging it is to realize that, no matter what went wrong in your life—no matter how early—God can set it right and set the captive—that is, you—free.

It was you who created my inmost self, and put me together in my mother's womb; for all these mysteries I thank you: for the wonder of myself, for the wonder of your works.

You know me through and through, from having watched my bones take shape when I was being formed in secret, knitted together in the limbo of the womb.

You had scrutinized my every action, all were recorded in your book, my days listed and determined, even before the first of them occurred *(Ps. 139:13–17).*

Chapter One

A BEAUTIFUL IDEAL:
FOR HUSBANDS AND WIVES
TO PRAY TOGETHER

(by Francis)

Since God has made husband and wife into one body,[1] there should be nothing more natural than for them to speak with God together. I want to emphasize (as we mentioned in the introduction) that only a tiny minority of Christian husbands and wives pray together, and even fewer *(perhaps only 1 percent)* pray together for their unborn children.

Christian marriages have really been robbed of their heritage—so thoroughly robbed that they don't even know what they are missing!

So, Judith and I want to share our discoveries about what prayer can do to create unity between husband and wife. Something really does happen when we pray for each other. In my earlier book, *The Prayer that Heals,*[2] I tried to encourage ordinary people to pray at home for healing, because they need to learn that beautiful things will happen once they begin to pray together. Jesus tried so hard to encourage people to pray when he said:

> "Is there anyone among you who would hand his son a stone when he asked for bread? Or would hand him a snake when he asked for a fish? If you, then, evil as you are, know how to give your children what is good, how much more will your Father in heaven give good things to those who ask him!" *(Mt.* 7:9–11, NJB)

Jesus is clearly telling you that, no matter how much you love your children, his Father—now *your* Father—loves you far more! If you ask, He *will* answer. "Ask and you will receive, and so your joy will be complete" *(Jn.* 16:24). Do you dare believe how much God loves you? Jesus is saying that God will answer your prayers even though you still have areas of evil in your life ("If you, then, evil as you are . . ."); you can trust your loving Father who truly wants you to ask for good things.

One afternoon, while Judith was nursing and rocking our newborn Rachel, she was overwhelmed as she gazed at the baby's beauty. She couldn't believe she could love anyone so much! And she realized that her love wasn't selfish. As she looked, she heard God's voice within her say:

"You love her very much, don't you?"

Judith replied:

"Oh yes, you know I do."

To which God responded:

"I love you *more* than you love Rachel."

But she couldn't accept that:

"Oh, no you don't. You couldn't!"

(She *knew* that she loved Rachel, but she had not yet experienced the fullness of God's love for her.)

God gently answered:

"Oh, yes I do!"

When she heard that voice within her, the realization of God's love suffused her heart and Judith began to cry for joy; she had never experienced the Father's love for her at this depth. It was as if Judith needed a child of her own to love before she could feel God's love for her to the utmost.

Both Judith and I have experienced God's love and seen so many prayers answered:

> What we have seen and heard we are telling you
> so that you too may be in union with us, as we are
> in union with the Father and with his Son Jesus
> Christ. We are writing this to you to make our own
> joy complete (I *Jn.* 1:3–4).

As we experience healing taking place over and over when we pray, our hope is strengthened the next time we pray. Even though faith "prove the existence of realities that are unseen" *(Heb.* 11:1, NJB), our weak humanity is helped by our having "seen" healings and miracles of God's provision. These past blessings build up our certainty that God hears us when we pray for the unborn child, who is so totally dependent on the love and mercy of God.

Tiny John the Baptist, in only his sixth month in Elizabeth's womb, responded with a leap to the presence of Jesus:

> . . . as soon as Elizabeth heard Mary's greeting, the child *leapt in her womb* and Elizabeth was filled with the Holy Spirit. She gave a loud cry and said, "Of all women you are the most blessed, and blessed is the fruit of your womb. Why should I be honored with a visit from the mother of my Lord? Look, the moment your greeting reached my ears, the child in my womb *leapt for joy*" (*Lk.* 1:41–44, NJB. Italics added.)

Not only did John the Baptist sense Jesus' presence, but, even at that age, he responded emotionally, with joy! Psychologists now corroborate what Luke describes: your unborn child can respond to you emotionally. He can feel love, fear, rejection and joy. Already, floating in your womb, he is beginning to love life, or, on the other hand, is starting to fear life and move toward spiritual death. Once you realize how much you can help your unborn babe by praying, you will be as eager to pray every day as you are careful to watch over your diet to make sure your baby is well nourished. And, just as husbands are learning to share in the birth process by taking natural-child-birth classes with their wives, so they can learn the delight of praying together for their baby's happiness—for God to shed his blessings and love upon that unborn child.

If so much good results when we pray together why is it that more married people don't try it? For one thing, we know that it's hard for married couples to get started praying together. Somehow, prayer is such a *personal* matter that it actually seems harder for most married people to pray together than to have sexual relations. We often seem *ashamed* of praying together; we are afraid of opening up our inmost self to another human being—especially to our married partner who knows us in our worst unspiritual moments. We know of a psychologist who was conducting a survey of married couples to find out about their attitudes on key problems. In the survey, he asked one hundred questions; in them were hidden the questions he was really interested in. When he got near the hundredth question, he was just grasping to fill up his list, so he added "Do you ever pray together?" almost as an afterthought. To his surprise, the couples freely answered the most intimate questions about their finances and about physical details of their sex lives. But when he got to the question about praying together, he was astonished by their usual response: "How dare you get so personal!"

Yet, if we can overcome our initial reluctance and get started praying together, a wonderful world of love and communication will open up to us. In some mysterious way, we find that by talking to Jesus (and to his Father) together, we somehow are drawn closer to each other. These moments of union with God will also be among our most intimate experiences of union with our married partner.

Even if, as a couple, you can't make the step of praying together, the mother can still pray alone; she can still do most of the things we recommend in this book. She can place her hand on her abdomen as close as she can to her little baby. Even though her husband isn't present, she is not alone; she is praying in God's presence with her child. And, somehow, her baby can respond. Our friend, Dr. Conrad Baars described how this can be done:

"A woman who is four-and-a-half or five months pregnant (or more) should gently put her hands on her abdomen, one on the right side of her womb, the other on the left. By leaving them there in the same position and without exerting pressure, she can cause the child in the womb to move from one side to the other. Thus, she can gently 'rock' the child from left to right and from right to left.

"How does the woman do this? How does she communicate with her child?

"What the mother actually does is nothing more than being present to the child in her womb with the full attention of her whole being. As she imagines it growing and living there in all its innocence and goodness, her feeling of tender love awakens and increases. If she wishes to touch and caress her child with her love, she can do so by letting her feeling of love flow into one of her hands, let us say the right one. In doing so, she may or may not become more aware of the sensation of touch in her right hand as it gently rests on her abdomen.

"Before long, she will notice the child moving inside of her womb. It swims to the part of its temporary 'home' where the right hand of its mother lies. The child nestles as it were with its back in the hollow of its mother's loving hand, somewhat like the little child does in the beautiful carving, illustrating the prophet's words, 'See, upon the palms of my hands I have written your name' *(Is.* 49:16).

"When she now directs her feeling of love to her left hand, the child after a while will sense this and swim to the other side of the uterus to nestle in the hollow of its mother's left hand. The mother 'rocks' her child, swimming in the amniotic fluid . . . extending her feelings of love now to one hand, then to the other.

"How is it possible? In some mysterious way . . . the child senses this force emanating from the mother, and responds by moving toward the spot where it enters its little fluid world. Mother and child give and receive in an interplay of love, a first for the child, months before it is ready to be born. The mother gives, and the child receives in return by actively receiving and responding to the mother's tender, but unspoken, sentiment: 'It is good that you are here; I love to be with you; I love to play with you.' And so the child 'says' to the mother, 'It is good to feel your loving presence; you make me feel wanted and worthwhile; it is good to be part of you.'

"That this exchange of love is most important to the unborn child becomes evident when the mother—and for that matter the father, too—has made it a practice to be present to their child in this affirming way every day at a certain time. If, for some reason, she skips one of these regular 'visits,' the child will react by kicking against the wall of its 'home.' It does not like to be ignored, and reminds its mother that it needs and wants to feel her love!

"During the last weeks of her pregnancy the mother, in playing with her unborn child, can make it grow familiar with the birth canal, so that it will know which way it must leave the womb. During the process of labor and delivery, mother and father should continue to be present to the child and guide it gently through the birth canal. Through this continued loving presence of the parents to the child the labor pains are continually reduced and the delivery becomes that much easier."[3]

What Dr. Baars is speaking about, of course, is the communication of human love through touch; but prayer adds a dimension of *God's love* which is communicated along with the mother's (and father's) love. As we know, one of the channels of God's healing power is *touch,* and Jesus often healed the sick by simply touching them:

> At sunset all those who had friends suffering
> from diseases of one kind or another brought them
> to him, and laying his hands on each he cured
> them *(Lk.* 4:40).

Even without words, our touch is a kind of prayer of the heart, communicating God's love and power.[4] The woman with an issue of blood decided, "If I can touch his clothes I shall be well again." As soon as she touched the hem of Jesus' garment, the woman was cured. "Immediately aware that power had gone out from him, Jesus turned around in the crowd and said, 'Who touched my clothes?' " *(Mk. 5:30)*

Since so few of us ever saw our own parents praying together in nonformal ways, we need some kind of model of how to pray. Actually, it's very easy.

The way Judith and I prayed for our children before they were born was very simple. We chose to pray twice a day: once after breakfast, before I left for the office; the other time was the last thing at night, lying in bed before going to sleep.

In the morning we would share a reading of Scripture (after Rachel was born we dropped this because she demanded our attention and our time of prayer together had to be shortened). We would also read a commentary on the day's Scripture and then discuss it together.[5] After praying in gratitude for God's recent blessings we would also pray for protection against evil—from Satan, from sickness, from accidents and from all harm. In short, "Deliver us from evil." Then we would pray for each other, for all our individual needs—especially if something was coming up that day where we realized we needed God's special help.

Next, we would place our hands on Judith's tummy and pray. Following the growth of our baby as best we could (by reading about the development of embryos in utero[6]), we then asked God to perfectly form the heart, the blood system, the fingers and toes or whatever other parts of the body were being formed in secret:

> Your own hands shaped me, modeled me . . .
> You modeled me, remember, as clay is modeled
> . . . Did you not pour me out like milk, and cur-
> dle me then like cheese;[7] clothe me with skin and

flesh, and weave me of bone and sinew? *(Jb.* 10:8–11)

We asked Jesus to guide that growth perfectly; we asked him to fill our little baby with his life and with his love to its fullest capacity. Just as we had prayed for ourselves, we asked Jesus to protect our baby from all harm—from any accident and from any evil influence. (From time to time, we also prayed in the ways we shall describe in the coming chapters.)

And we prayed also for Judith: we prayed for the days she felt tired—when she felt sick—we prayed for her strength and encouragement—and for a happy day of birth. We were helplessly aware that, beyond a point, there was nothing we could do but wait.

AND TRUST GOD.

Our great desire is simply to encourage you to pray for your unborn child and to know that your prayer will make a difference. Friends who learned late in their marriages to pray for their unborn child, have often shared with us something like this: "This last child, our fourth, is really different. From the moment she was born she seems to have been more peaceful, more joyful than the others. The other children are wonderful, too—it's not that. It's just that this child is specially blest!"

Shortly after I had written the above paragraph, I received a letter from a couple confirming the experience of so many other parents. Several years ago they had read an article we had written on praying for the unborn child,[8] and then they put it into practice.

"At that time, our daughter, Jenny, was three years old," their letter said. "We explained to her that her new baby brother or sister could hear her, so she needed to be loving and talk to the baby. She would come up and kiss and hug my stomach and whisper little hellos to the baby. All of us would pray over the baby and Jenny would say her own simple and very beautiful prayers.

"Each day we took time to talk and pray with our baby. This was our prayer: 'Dear Lord, we ask you to bless and protect our baby, to fill it with your love, your peace and your joy—to surround this little baby with the warmth of your love. We ask you to help it grow and develop into the beautiful child you want it to be. Thank you for this baby and for blessing us and entrusting us with this new life.'

"As mother of our new baby, I made a conscious effort to avoid any stressful situations and to protect the baby. But there were times when I was angry, depressed and upset. As I got in touch with those feelings within me, I would begin to pray. I would apologize to the baby and try to explain what happened and then ask the Lord to heal those memories in the baby. I would pray that the Lord would replace any confusion or hurt or fear with his healing love. Then I would just hold my hands on my stomach over the baby and silently let the Lord's love flow through me to the baby.

"The difference in the two pregnancies was tremendous. Through the pregnancy with Jenny, I was sick most of the nine months. Labor and delivery were long and hard. (We didn't think of praying in those days.) The pregnancy with Albert was much better physically—and much more peaceful. We used the birthing room at the hospital, which added to the relaxed atmosphere. But, most important, Jenny was allowed to come in right after Albert was born and we spent time bonding together as a family. It was very special! Albert just looked around and was very peaceful and content. He seemed to recognize each of our voices, especially Jenny's.

"As the days and weeks went by, we noticed how happy

and peaceful he was, and, to our surprise, others also commented on Albert's joyful personality. Finally, we realized that our praying for Albert in the womb accounted for his peaceful, pleasant personality.

"Now he is a year and a half old; his personality is still joyful and peaceful. We still continue to bless and pray for each of our children every day, and the Lord continues to bless us all."

Chapter Two

PREPARING FOR BIRTH

(by Judith)

Along with the thrill of pregnancy comes your transformation
from a couple into a family. Every level of your life will be
touched and forever changed by the new experience of being a
mother or father. No other event in your life will have the
power to carve within you such depths of love and joy; but along
with that happiness will come fear and need. As we look back
now, we marvel at the changes that have resulted in our life as a
couple ever since we had our two little ones. How they fill our
lives and challenge us to grow! Out of this challenge to love,
guide and discipline them we have learned to rely on our Father in Heaven—and upon each other. We spend much of our

time communicating our concerns, questions and needs to each other. Then we pray for God's help.

Communication is absolutely necessary in the life of a family, whether it be two people or fourteen people. Communication is as necessary for the life of a relationship as blood is for the body. In my work as a therapist, I have seen the miracle of broken families being restored through communication and prayer. I know of no other time when communication is more needed than during pregnancy and childbirth. Ideally, this communication started even before you committed your lives to one another and became one in marriage. But, if it didn't begin back then, the union you feel when your child is conceived is an ideal time to begin sharing your hearts—your dreams, your fears and your needs.

Because of our knowledge about the importance of the child's prenatal development, we decided to do everything possible to aid in the well-being of our children. This included my eating properly, resting, exercising, praying and preparing for a natural delivery. We took Lamaze classes, and spent much time together practicing breathing exercises. We must have read almost all the books on childbirth, including the inspiring book *Birth Without Violence.*[1] We saw films of actual births and wept openly together as we sat with our class on pillows on the floor of the hospital—experiencing together the beauty and miracle of birth and life. However, no single book, lecture, film or talking with "experienced" parents prepared us for the awesome experience of bringing forth our own little Rachel! Never before had we, as a couple, reached such complete oneness as we did in helping her make her passage into our waiting arms. It was a long labor, due to her turned position, so we had many hours to spend (from 4 A.M. to 5 P.M.) sharing, working, laughing, praying and finally weeping with great joy when we saw her for the first time. One of the purposes of natural childbirth is to help the parents-to-be work as a team. I marveled at the process of birth, but equally important to me was the oneness with Francis which enabled him to sense and anticipate my fears, pain or loss of control. He would then gently encourage me to remain relaxed and, with his help, to regain control through prayer and rhythmic breathing. Our oneness was such a source of strength that, when "transition" came and everything started moving so fast, I felt steadied. His presence, holding my hand and praying while I looked into his peaceful eyes, allowed me to draw from him courage and strength to complete the birth. This unspoken level of communication, which can only be communicated by touch and with the eyes, was not attained overnight. It had been worked at and refined since we first met. Then, with our marriage, we had the time to reflect on our love as a gift from God by spending long hours sharing and praying together. This whole discovery of each other intensified when Rachel, our first child, was conceived. We're so thankful we had built this mutual closeness and trust as a preparation for experiencing the birth process.

Most couples think of these nine months as the most joyful time of their lives; and so they are. The joyful anticipation of life, the plans for the baby, choosing a name, preparing a nursery, the layette, the showers and parties, being the center of attention wherever you go. All very exciting. But, as with all things in life, there is another side, a shadow side, that can fester and grow if left in the darkness. Those fears, feelings of loneliness, anxieties, mood swings, nausea all need to be discussed and prayed about with your husband—or with a close friend.

It was difficult in the beginning of the pregnancy to share our fears and needs, but we're so thankful we did, because they intensified as the birth grew near. Would I be able to handle the birth without anesthetic? Would I be a good mother? And so many more anxieties and questions.

We have counseled and prayed with many other couples who have experienced the heights and depths of emotion waiting for their baby. The husband is usually very confused by his wife's mood swings and her puzzling personality changes. Some women go from being very carefree and funloving to becoming serious when they realize the awesome responsibility of becoming a mother. (I know that I did!) The hormonal changes taking place in the mother-to-be can also be very confusing—and sometimes frightening as well. Some women become deeply depressed and increasingly concerned about whether they are ready to be a mother.

Much of their depression can be attributed to the hormonal and chemical changes taking place because of pregnancy and lactation. Some moms-to-be have said to me, "I feel so crazy some days; one moment I'm ecstatic with joy and the world is a beautiful place; the next moment I wonder what I'm doing bringing a child into this world!" Or, "Sometimes I love the changes in my body and I think I'm beautiful, but at other times, I feel as if I'm just plain clumsy and ugly." The nausea some women experience makes the first three months (or sometimes, the entire pregnancy) hard to enjoy. One beautiful older mother was coming to me for counseling. She experienced severe nausea for nine months, so much so that, on the days when I knew she was coming to my office, I was very careful not to use perfume or have any sprays or smells that might make her sick. One day, when she looked especially green and had spent most of the hour lying on the couch, I asked her how she felt about her baby. She lit up (through her green face) and said she was thrilled to be carrying the little one and didn't mind at all the discomfort she was going through. I want to add that the whole family, including her teenage children, pitched in to support and help her. This pregnancy, which might have been a terrible experience, turned into an opportunity for the entire family to grow in love, patience and understanding.

While most nausea is hormonally or chemically induced, studies indicate that some nausea can be attributed to an unconscious conflict concerning the baby or becoming a parent. This conflict, if left unresolved through lack of communication and prayer, can cause emotional and physical distress which may eventually affect your baby. This conflict can be due to fears which have remained dormant until pregnancy.

One of the common fears is the most basic of all: becoming a mother. Some women, from the time they were small girls playing house, have envisioned themselves becoming a wife and mother. For them, the transition is a very natural, easy one. They probably grew up in a large family where lots of babies were around, so they feel comfortable with a newborn. For others, like myself, changing a diaper was a totally new experience, not to mention holding, bathing, feeding and all of the other activities required in caring for a new baby. I'll never forget how, shortly after Rachel was born, she had a B.M. in our hospital room and we had to change her. I, being the mother, was supposed to be the expert. Francis was helping when, suddenly, we both looked at each other and managed to laugh, confessing that neither one of us had ever changed a diaper before.

Being a mother or a father can be a very frightening experience. Conflicts can be specially severe if the experience you had with your own mother or father was negative or painful. One woman I counseled was afraid of becoming pregnant because of some very wounding experiences she had had with her father. She was afraid that the very same thing would happen to any children she might have. I asked her to forgive her father, and I prayed for Jesus to heal the memories of those painful experiences. (She conceived a child shortly after our prayers and had a wonderful pregnancy and delivery.)

I remember when my mother and father heard the news of the birth of their first grandchild. My father said, "I don't mind being a grandfather, but I'm not sure I want to be married to a grandmother." This expresses what some husbands feel when they see the changes that take place in their wives. Men always treat pregnant women differently, so pregnant wives need not be surprised when their husbands change in relation to them. Some husbands show extra concern and care, while others seem to reject their wives in one way or the other. One pregnant woman told me that her husband had stopped making love with her. When I talked to him about it, he finally confessed he hadn't lost his desire for her—he was just afraid he might hurt her. When the couple talked about it she came to see that what she had originally perceived as a rejection was really a reflection of his love and concern. The changes become even more profound after the baby's birth, so it is absolutely necessary for the couple to keep the channels of communication open during pregnancy. They need to try to understand and support each other at all times, but especially so during pregnancy. These times of deep change will be lonely times if they are not shared. This is especially true for the pregnant mother—so many changes are going on in her body, and in the way her husband, friends and parents relate to her.

It should be clear that the husband has great potential to be a most important influence on his wife. By supporting and consistently affirming her, he can make a tremendous difference in her happiness. And this, in turn, will influence the well-being of their little baby. When doubts, fear or insecurities come, he can dispel them all with words of encouragement and a listening heart.

He especially needs to reassure her about the birth process itself. How many women have said to us, "I wonder if I'll do all right"? Or, "Maybe I'll make a fool of myself by screaming or shouting." Many mothers-to-be, especially first-time mothers, fear the birth process. So many horror stories abound, describing long, traumatic labors, usually told by older mothers who don't realize the effect it is having on the mom-to-be. Even your own mother may have told you stories about how she birthed you and how much pain you caused her. She may have made you feel guilty about causing her so much pain. I've prayed with several women who feared giving birth because of stories their mothers told them. Sometimes this fear can be so intense it actually seems to block conception. Or it interferes with natural birth. We recently talked with one father-to-be who said his wife is so afraid of birth that she is already planning what anesthesia she will use. She won't even consider natural childbirth. This is sad; her fear is preventing the woman from feeling and experiencing the miracle of the baby coming forth from her body. When a woman is so wrapped up in fear due to her past memories or experiences we need to pray for inner healing. One of my best friends has a mother who is always reminding her how much pain and damage she caused her during the birth. Needless to say, both my friend and her mother stand in great need of prayer for healing.

In contrast, I like the way one of our friends described the birth of her three sons when I asked if it was painful. I had been reading books on childbirth without pain, but I wasn't completely convinced they were true. She looked mildly surprised that I had asked the question and said she never considered it to be pain, just hard work! How right she was! We discovered why it's called Labor when we had our first child. It was definitely a lot of work for everyone involved, but what a rich reward. The words of Jesus are so true and beautiful:

> A woman in childbirth suffers, because her time has come; but when she has given birth to the child she forgets the suffering in her joy that a human being has been born into the world *(Jn.* 16:21, NJB).

Giving birth should be a powerful spiritual and emotional experience for both the mother and the father. We need to enter into this experience to our fullest. Physically, unless complications exist, the baby and the mother are completely prepared by God for the precious time of coming forth. Nothing in life will find you so prepared as giving birth. I still marvel at the miracle of birth—how every part of my body was made ready for that moment. We have several friends who are obstetricians and midwives who tell us how the harmony of the birth process still impresses them as a miracle. One man we know was an atheist until he witnessed the birth of his first child. He wept openly for the first time in his life when he beheld the miracle of life. You truly become aware of the hand of the Creator when you experience a birth.

If you realize that your body is perfectly prepared for giving life, and you pray, study and exercise as the birthday approaches, you should have a steady confidence as you reach that special date. As for those fears you still have, try to share them with your husband, and pray for any encouragement and healing you may still need.

Lately we find so much concern in parents-to-be about the physical well-being of their coming child. We know of parents who take regular sonograms to check their unborn baby's physical condition. Their attitude is: "If our baby isn't perfect, we don't want it!" Their idea of perfection—stressing the physical—is, in itself, imperfect. Their fears are obviously excessive, and most parents will not go to those extremes. Still, our concerns will always be there, until we hold our baby, count the fingers and toes and examine her entire body. But, even should the child be physically imperfect, healing prayer, even before birth, is the Christian's answer—not abortion. Nor need physical imperfections hinder our child's spiritual growth or happiness upon this earth.

Nevertheless, being older parents, we spent a good portion of our prayer time focused on the physical and mental well-being of our babies. During our last pregnancy, because I was to be thirty-five years old when David was born, my obstetrician advised us to have genetic counseling. We discussed it, prayed about it and decided against it because we knew we wouldn't abort the fetus even if something was wrong. We continued in prayer; if at any time fears crept into us, we would discuss them, and ask our Father in Heaven to give us his peace.

This is one area where the love of supportive friends and the prayers of fellow Christians can be tremendous sources of strength and hope. Our friends loved and prayed for our little ones long before they saw or held them. There is a very special bond which exists between our children and the members of our prayer group. Every stage of our children's development during pregnancy and birth was monitored and prayed for by our prayer group. During labor at the hospital, several friends were in the waiting room praying and sending in notes and words of encouragement. Some even came into the birthing suite and helped me with my breathing; they prayed with me and encouraged me. A real celebration of life occurred after each birth. The love of our friends and their prayers still continue to bless our family on a regular basis. When Rachel or David falls sick or the load grows too heavy, all we need to do is go to the phone, and our friends start praying immediately. Sometimes, friends appear at the door, guided by love and by the Holy Spirit, to pray for us and help us. As I'm writing this now, several friends have called today to see how my father is feeling.[2] They, without knowing him personally, have been interceding for ten weeks for his healing. At times, several of our friends wake up in the middle of the night under the strong impression that we need prayer. And they are always right! This is the kind of prayer support and love we all need, especially at times when our lives change so rapidly.

Many times during my pregnancies, Francis and I would read Scripture to one another, and to the baby within. It had a very calming effect in bringing us back to the reality that the little one I was carrying was really God's child, and very much in his plan and care. I especially enjoyed meditating on Psalm 139, allowing the Spirit to show me God's hand, knitting together and forming our baby. I could sense God's presence within me, keeping our little one enveloped in his love and light.

> You know me through and through, from having watched my bones take shape when I was being formed in secret, knitted together in the limbo of the womb.
> You have scrutinized my every action, all were recorded in your book, my days listed and determined, even before the first of them occurred *(Ps. 139:15–17)*.

Chapter Three

AT THE BEGINNING
(Praying to Conceive)

(by Francis)

The Word of Yahweh was addressed to me saying:

> "Before I formed you in the womb I knew you;
> before you came to birth I consecrated you;
> I appointed you as a prophet to the nations" *(Jer.
> 1:4–5)*.

In a very special way, God knew Jeremiah and called him—
even *before* he was conceived. We, too—every one of us—have
been known and chosen by God, even before our parents came
together. Humanly speaking, some children may be accidents

—their parents may not have planned or wanted them—but, in God's eyes, no child is a mistake. We were all desired and created by God, even when our earthly parents did not want us.

Amazingly, one of the prayers that has *almost always* been answered in our ministry has been when we have prayed for husbands and wives who haven't been able to conceive. For many years, it seemed that every time we prayed for a couple to conceive a child, they did. And often the child was born nine months after the prayer.

Lately, we have found a few exceptions, when couples have not succeeded in conceiving, but usually our prayer has been answered. God seems to delight in bringing forth new life when we ask him.

In the Bible we find many examples of infertile couples giving birth unexpectedly in old age—a special, unexpected blessing of God. In fact, the barren-woman-conceiving is one of the major themes of the Bible:

> Shout for joy, you barren women who bore no children! Break into cries of joy and gladness, you who were never in labor! For the sons of the forsaken one are more in number than the sons of the wedded wife, says Yahweh *(Is.* 54:1).

God's miraculous assistance in helping barren couples conceive starts all the way back in *Genesis* with Sarah and Abraham:

> Now Abraham and Sarah were old, well on in years, and Sarah had ceased to have her monthly periods. So Sarah laughed to herself, thinking, "Now that I am past the age of child-bearing, and my husband is an old man, is pleasure to come my way again!"

But Yahweh asked Abraham, "Why did Sarah laugh and say, 'Am I really going to have a child now that I am old?' Nothing is impossible for Yahweh? I shall come back to you at the same time next year and Sarah will have a son" *(Gn.* 18:11–14, NJB).

God's helping the barren woman conceive is a strand woven throughout the Old Testament (for instance, the barren Hannah conceives the future prophet Samuel (1 *S.* 1:20–21) and it continues on into the New Testament when the elderly, child-less Elizabeth conceives John the Baptist *(Lk.* 1:11–25), "for nothing is impossible to God" *(Lk.* 1:37). This miraculous assis-tance culminates, of course, in the virgin Mary being overshad-owed by the Holy Spirit and conceiving the Messiah, Jesus *(Lk.* 1:26–38).

God is very much on the side of life—new life in particular! So, if you want children, but haven't been able to have them, pray and ask God to help create new life within you.

Here is how it happened to one woman:

"I don't know if you remember my husband and me—you prayed for us in June '82. If you recall, the doctors told me that my chances of having a baby were only 10 percent due to a uterine disease. I had surgery and we had been trying ever since. I had gone through all the medication, tests and agony for almost two years.

"You told us that, in your experience, God almost always healed this kind of situation. Well, that was in June. In August, the doctors told me I would have to have surgery again, with a possible hysterectomy. I fell to pieces! The surgery was set for December. The next couple of months we prayed in agony . . .

"Then the Lord answered my prayers with a big "YES." In

November, I got pregnant. It was my *last* chance before surgery. The doctors then told me that they had only told me that I had a 10 percent chance [to conceive] in order to make me feel better. They were amazed.

"On June 10, 1983, I gave birth to a cute baby: David Edward! He was born early but was a good size, weighing 6 pounds, 11 ounces."

As you can gather, we are delighted whenever a barren couple asks us to pray that they might have a baby. But even for those who conceive easily, praying in preparation is vital. Let me share several things we have learned about that.

First, we realize that marriage is holy. In churches of Catholic tradition, marriage is a sacrament, a visible sign to us of God's invisible love. Tragically many Christians feel that sex is somehow dirty and have separated out this part of their lives from their experience of God. For example, for centuries, the Church taught that married couples were soiled by the marriage act and could not receive communion the day after having had sexual relations. St. Gregory the Great, one of the eight "Great Doctors" of the Church, taught that a couple could no more expect to have relations and not sin than they could hold their hands in a flame and not be burned.[1] Christian attitudes have changed but, deep down, some of this suspicion—that there is entirely too much pleasure involved for the marriage act to be suitable for a mortified Christian—still remains in the subconscious of some married people.

But if they truly understand that marriage is holy in its sexual aspects, a Christian couple should feel very right, very comfortable about praying with each other before making love. And, if they want to conceive, they can also ask God to bless their intercourse with a new child.

We have a friend who believes that, according to God's original plan (before the Fall of Adam and Eve), men and

women were meant to be so totally integrated on every level—
their spirits, emotions and bodies working in such perfect harmony—that they would never even think of joining their bodies
sexually unless they were already united at the spiritual level. In
this ideal state, their very act of sexual union would constitute
the marriage—a sign that they were already spiritually one.
Only after the Fall, when our emotions, our minds, our wills and
our spirits tended to go their own unruly ways, do we find it
necessary to bind up our marriages by a written, legal contract.[2]
Furthermore, in God's original plan, we would be so united—
one flesh and one spirit—that we would never think of divorc-
ing. As Jesus said:

> "Have you not read that the Creator from the
> beginning 'made them male and female,' and that
> he said: 'This is why a man leaves his father and
> mother and becomes attached to his wife, and the
> two become one flesh?' They are no longer two,
> therefore, but one flesh. So then, what God has
> united, human beings must not divide" *(Mt.* 19:4–
> 6, NJB).

So, the very union of our bodies is meant to be a visible sign
of the interior joining together of our spirits: union at every
level is at the heart of marriage. Ideally, there should be no
need for a spoken or written legal contract. Yet, in our fallen
nature we now need the legal knot because, so often, our spiritual union is weak. "In my inmost self I dearly love God's Law,
but I can see that my body follows a different law that battles
against the law which my reason dictates" *(Rm.* 7:22).

There is, of course, no way of proving that our friend's
theory is true, but it does make a lot of sense. What is certain is
that the time when a husband and wife experience their greatest physical union can also be a time when they pray and experi-

ence their union with God to the utmost. If we want to conceive a child, why shouldn't we pray—especially before making love?

Another universal Christian tradition says that our marriage is meant to be an image of the intimate life of God; the love between Father and Son is so great that it calls forth a third person, the Holy Spirit. The Spirit has always been seen as reflecting God's creative *love* in a special way. Similarly, the love between husband and wife is so strong that it generates a third person, that little baby who is a sign of our love for each other. Every new baby we conceive, then, is a reflection of the Holy Spirit—a sign of God's love—and, at the same time, of our love for each other!

PREPARING OURSELVES
FOR CONCEPTION

If, in the ideal order, we should pray for new life at the time we make love in the hopes of conceiving, we also need to prepare our hearts to be wholly in favor of having a baby at this time. Seldom are parents fully desirous of bringing a new baby into this world. Usually they experience at least *some* reluctance to having a child and harbor thoughts such as, "Do we really have enough money to support another child?" There is an old saying, "I was born in the Great Depression, and I've been depressed ever since." (Apparently there is a grain of truth in this, since parents, at that time, were often of a double mind about having a child.) Or they may think in their inmost heart, "Do I really want to go through those sleepless nights all over again?" Is the mother ready to undergo morning sickness, the unpredictable mood swings and the pain of birth, together with the uncertainty about whether the baby will be normal—especially when she draws toward the end of her childbearing years?

Here is the story of one woman who was ambivalent about conceiving a child, of the damage that her reluctance caused and of the eventual healing of her wounded relationship with God, her husband and her child:

"Back during the Vietnam War, my husband was high on the list to be drafted. He was greatly afraid he might be killed, so he asked me to get pregnant so he could get a paternity deferment. My heart anguished for I loved and wanted to please him, but I also wanted to fulfill my dream of becoming a nurse. I did become pregnant but was ambivalent about it, and I did not love the child in my womb. When my son, John, was eventually born, we found that he had a handicap; he is somewhat retarded and was a very difficult baby to take care of.

"When my husband had to go for his Army physical, he was given a *medical* deferment. You can imagine my anger and resentment. I was so angry with God that I had been given this burden for nothing! I was filled with self-pity. This was the beginning of many years of marital strife. Our problems became so acute that we went to see Frank and Susan, a couple we trusted, for counsel. One day they came to our home to share dinner. When Frank met John, he burst into tears and exclaimed, 'What a blessing this child is!' I was so shocked and thought, 'A blessing?' How such a small thing was to change my whole life! Slowly I began to see what a blessing John was to me, and to all of us. Yet, in many ways I still kept wounding him, while, in return, he loved me more and just accepted me . . .

"Then I attended your conference and after one of Judith's presentations I asked my small community to pray with me and I then experienced such a healing! I saw Jesus take a seed from his heart and he held it out to me in his cupped hand. His face was so *full of love.* The seed glowed with light. I took it and saw myself pregnant. Next Jesus was walking with me and the angels were singing to John and telling him how much he was loved. I asked Jesus to give John all that I was not able to give him. Then I saw myself in the delivery room and Jesus delivered my son—my own dear son—and handed him to me, and I just took him to my bosom with such love.

"I couldn't wait to call home, and John answered the phone and asked me if I would be home soon. I could only say, 'I love you, and I can't wait to get home.' Praise the Lord that I could be so touched and healed."

This true story is a beautiful example of how God can redeem our past mistakes. But how much better it would be if we could only learn to avoid mistakes by communicating our real beliefs, thoughts and feelings to our partner. We need to share, as best we can, our fears as well as our hopes, our dark side as well as our light. Then we can make our fears the subject of our prayer together so that we can share each other's strengths and pray for each other's burdens. We must cleanse our hearts to be the parents our baby will need—we need to love our child unconditionally. Of course, we will never be able to do this perfectly, but we do the best we can: ". . . I am far from thinking that I have already won. All I can say is that I forget the past and I strain ahead for what is still to come" *(Ph.* 3:13).

We want to welcome this new life, whether it be a boy or girl, whether it be a genius or retarded, whether it be perfectly formed or, in some way, physically misshapen. Perhaps the cruelest thing that can happen to a child is to discover that he is a basic mistake in the eyes of his parents—that they didn't really want him.[3] If his mom and dad, the very ones who know him the best, don't really want him, don't love him, how can the child grow up to believe that anyone else could ever really love him? His little house is built on shifting sand. The greatest gift we can give our children is our own unconditional willing them into existence. Our love is only a pale reflection of God's love, but still we know that our love is a channel of God's own love for our baby. Our hatred of life can block that channel and prevent God's love from getting through.

Sometimes our past is the block that keeps us from whole-heartedly desiring a child. The woman may, for example, be afraid of giving birth because of what her own mother has told her about how much pain she went through in giving birth. Or she may have had a miscarriage and now fears whether she might not miscarry again. When the wife harbors these fearful attitudes (often through no fault of her own), she can share them with her husband (or with a close friend) and ask him to pray with her for the inner healing she needs to prepare herself to conceive. So, we need to pray for inner healing about any past experiences that have clouded our appreciation of the miracle of birth and our willingness to sacrifice comfort and sleep in order to see a tiny new baby into the light of this world.

If we pray, too, asking God to help us choose the right time to conceive and to bless our union at the time we make love, we can be amazingly in tune with the miracle of birth. Judith was so in touch with what was happening in her body that she felt sure when Rachel (born August 2, 1981) was conceived; in fact, that very next morning we prayed together for that little life that God had brought into existence through our love. With David (nineteen months later) she wasn't so sure, although she was sure enough that she changed her eating and drinking habits the following day so that her body might more easily carry a new baby.

INNER HEALING OF
OUR OWN CONCEPTION

Often, when we read about another person's problems, we suddenly recognize our own need for healing. So, in reading this, you may have become aware of something that was missing when your parents conceived you. According to British psychiatrist Dr. Frank Lake, his clients show an amazing ability to sense how their mothers and fathers felt about themselves. Often they can vividly reconstruct their parents' relationship within which they were conceived.[4]

Perhaps you suspect that there was violence when your mother and father came together; perhaps there was lust—a kind of violence—rather than love. Perhaps your mother was indifferent to the sex act and only submitted reluctantly, out of a sense of duty. Or perhaps your parents were not married and your conception was a surprise, an unwelcome shock. Or, again, your parents loved each other but didn't want a child at the time you arrived. So many different things can go wrong.

The good news is that, no matter what went wrong, Jesus can heal you. If you know that something was missing from the very beginning, you can pray and ask the Lord to take away the power of your past to hurt you.

Recently we received a beautiful testimony from an Episcopal priest about how he was healed of a wound that went all the way back to conception:

"Following the first talk on Wednesday, I went off by myself, as instructed. As I was rocking in one of the chairs on the porch, I became aware of a deep sorrow and began to cry softly. It is not like me to cry, so I knew something of considerable importance was happening to me. I felt the presence of Jesus. He said to me, "Read *Ephesians* . . ."

"I found myself accused and condemned at every turn by such things as, 'Lead a life worthy of the calling to which you have been called.' *(Ep.* 4:1) On I plunged through 'empty words,' 'sons of disobedience,' 'unfruitful works of darkness' to 'do not get drunk with wine *(Ep.* 5:6–18 passim, RSV) and I stopped abruptly.

" 'I stopped drinking anything alcoholic months ago,' I protested. Jesus said to me, 'I'm not accusing you of anything. You are! You think I wanted you to read this to accuse you, but I didn't. That's not who I am to you. I wanted you to see what it is that I am promising you; but you always change my promises to you into accusations. I am not your accuser; I love you.'

"By this time I was really crying, and the feeling of his friendship touched me so deeply that I knew I would never again experience him as anything but my friend.

" 'Do you remember when you were in your mother's womb?' he began again, as though he couldn't wait to press on to more. Some few months earlier he had made it clear to me that my mother and father had not wanted me. As he asked me the question, I found myself back in my mother's womb. Jesus was with me, helping me remember. My mother had become pregnant with me nine months after the birth of my older brother. He then led me through the following: My mother was terrified about telling my father that she was pregnant, knowing that he would be furious with her. When she could not disguise it any longer, she told him and he was so furious that he struck her in the face. There were many terrible arguments about my conception, neither my father nor my mother wanting me to be born. There was one time, as Jesus led me to recall, toward the end of my mother's pregnancy, when my father became so enraged that he struck my mother in the abdomen. I felt that blow and the death it intended, and knew that my father wanted me dead before I was born.

"Jesus said, 'I wanted you born. *I* wanted you in my world!' For the first time in my life I knew the depth of sorrow in my life and the joy of Jesus' wanting me . . .

"Now, for the first time in my whole life, I am free of an inner duplicity which has limited every relationship and accomplishment in my life. I had never been sure that I wanted to live, so I never was sure I wanted to succeed at anything. This, in the face of the fact that by more than a few person's assessments, I am considered to be a very able, productive person."

I also remember a young woman who had a miserable self-image and, in compensation, fed herself gluttonously. She was way overweight—which increased her self-hatred. This self-hatred led, in turn, to more overeating. She was caught in a vicious circle. Several times friends had prayed for her to cut down on her eating, but it had never helped too much. Then, one night, on a retreat, after I prayed for the group, she had a vision in which she "saw" the finger of God guiding one among many sperm to a particular ovum. Then she saw them unite. At that instant, she *knew* her conception was planned by God—that it was no mistake! And, in that moment, she was healed.

One indication that you may need healing for the moment of conception is if you have a recurring dream of *falling out of darkness.* In fact, on one retreat, two women were assigned as roommates who hadn't known each other before. Both of them were illegitimate and had been given up by their mothers for adoption. And both were ashamed of their past—a mutual past they came to discover as they shared with each other their fearsome dream of falling out of darkness. And God healed both of them on that retreat.

If you know, then, that something was missing at the very beginning of your life, you can pray and ask Jesus to change its effect upon you, so that your past can no longer hurt you. Your prayer might go something like this:

"Heavenly Father, creator of everything that lives, my creator, go back to my very beginning." Then ask God to release you from any harmful effects stemming from your conception and from anything wrong in your parents' relationship. Next, ask God to "Fill the moment of my conception with all the love and joy that you always wanted me to have. I know that you desired and planned my life with an everlasting love, stretching back to the very beginning of the world. Please let me know this in the very depths of my heart. Let me know how much you longed for me. In place of the darkness in my heart, fill me with your light and love. Free me from every feeling of rejection and worthlessness. Let me know beyond the shadow of a doubt that I am your child. Fill me with all the mother's and father's love that I so needed and missed. Let the very moment when I came to life be filled with your light and love."

IN SUMMARY

If you want a child, then prepare yourselves for that new life. Fill yourselves with as much of God's life and love for each other as you can. And let the time of your coming together be filled with such love, joy and peace that the baby to be born will know that he is desired from the start of his little life. He will have no dreams of falling out of darkness but will sense light and love going back as far back as he can remember—and beyond.

With God there is no mistake: every child is planned by the "Father of all light,"[5] even when, according to our human reckoning, the child is not planned or is a "mistake."

So pray, even before you conceive your child. Pray every day to be close to God and close to each other. Pray for the right time to conceive and look forward with joy to the life to come!

Then, as soon as you know a child is conceived—whether it be the next day or the next month when your doctor confirms that the missed monthly period really means a child is on the way, you can start to pray for your baby's life and health. Pray that God's love (and your love) pour into that little baby, so that he will feel welcome and at home in this world. Pray that he develop well and be free of sickness. And pray that he be filled with as much of the life and spirit of God as his little being can receive.

> Yahweh called me when I was in the womb, before my birth he had pronounced my name *(Is.* 49:1, NJB).

Chapter Four

PRAYING DURING
THE FIRST TRIMESTER

(by Francis)

At first glance, it may seem strange that we recommend that you start to pray regularly as soon as you know that a baby is on the way. In our culture today, so many people believe that the baby in the first months after conception is just a blob of tissue and hardly a human being at all.

Yet, Dr. Frank Lake, a British psychiatrist, found, in working with twelve hundred clients, that the origins of their main personality disorders and psychosomatic problems came from their experience during the first trimester within their mother's womb. He believes that if a mother is filled with joy when she finds that she is pregnant, the embryo, in its own way, experiences joy at being recognized, accepted and welcomed. On the other hand, if the mother is distressed at finding herself pregnant, the fetus may be filled with a "bitter, black flood." And if the mother's rejection is excessive, the fetus even comes to long for death.[1] Apparently, some miscarriages result when the embryo "decides" that this world is not a good, welcoming place to be.

Some medical experts—perhaps most—question whether the embryo, at this early time, can remember or experience much of anything, but other doctors (like Dr. Lake and Dr. Thomas Verny) believe that, in some mysterious way, the human embryo can remember and feel, even at the earliest stages of life.

Mothers in many cultures have sensed this for thousands of years. For example, as soon as Mary, the mother of Jesus, learned that she was pregnant, she came to visit her cousin Elizabeth;[2] she was simply doing what any good Jewish mother of her day would do; she was expected to go apart for a time and prepare herself for the birth by praying and meditating upon the Scriptures. The people of Mary's time helped the mother-to-be by relieving her of most of the burdens of work and sending her to a relative's home to be cared for while she prepared to bring forth her child.

Elizabeth was six months pregnant when Mary arrived, and Mary stayed for three months, until the time came for Elizabeth to give birth to John the Baptist *(Lk.* 1:56–67). Mary was following the wisdom of Jewish custom by going apart and preparing herself spiritually. Mothers two thousand years ago knew a wisdom that we are just rediscovering today.

Recently, we were talking with our friend, Dr. Luis Galindo, a physician who has spent recent years working with the poor. He told us that when he treats a baby who seems remarkably happy and unafraid of the doctor, he asks the mother why the child seems so peaceful and content. Almost always the mother tells him that she sang and talked to her baby while she carried him in her womb. In his experience, Dr. Galindo has found that the mother's love before birth makes a big difference in the future happiness of her child.

What does this say to expectant parents? First of all, we believe it is never too early for them to begin praying, even before the mother feels the baby's first kick. If the mother and father would only pray together once or twice a day, what a wonderful help that would be, not only for their own relationship but for the happiness of their baby. You can pray together, you can sing, you can read Scripture, you can place your hands upon mother's tummy, and let this laying on of hands be a channel for God's love—and yours—to flow into that little embryo.

We consecrated our children to God while they were still in the womb; we asked God the Father to accept them as his children and to protect them from all harm. You can easily do the same thing and consecrate your children as soon as possible. This kind of prayer is like a baptism of desire; there is no reason why God cannot bless and accept your child long before it is born.[3]

You might also get a book with pictures that show how the fetus develops. Then you can pray, month by month, for each part of your child as he develops in God's plan—for his tiny ears, his lungs and his little fingers and toes. Pray each day for God to protect your child from all accidents and that he develops normally.

The mother's and father's attitudes toward their baby seem to be the *most important* determinants in their child's future happiness. Parents should give top priority to creating a peaceful, harmonious environment for the mother. They can decide to devote half an hour a day to praying or singing to the child.

Or, they can simply be quiet and rest in the Lord. The mother's state of calm is picked up by her baby, and the music that the baby hears continues to be recognized after birth.[4]

The desire to have a child—on the father's part as well as the mother's—is vital. The children of accepting mothers are much healthier, emotionally and physically, than the offspring of rejecting mothers.

Dr. Gerhard Rottman did a fascinating study on mothers and their attitudes toward their babies and divided them into four groups.[5]

1) *Ideal* mothers, the ones who wanted their children, had the easiest pregnancies, the most trouble-free births and the healthiest babies.

2) Their opposite, *catastrophic* mothers, the ones who didn't want children, had the worst medical problems during pregnancy and birthing and bore the highest rate of premature, low-weight and emotionally disturbed children.

3) Then there were *ambivalent* mothers, who were outwardly happy about their pregnancies, but deep down had reservations about having a child. Their babies had a high rate of gastrointestinal and behavioral problems ("colicy" babies).

4) *Cool* mothers had conscious reasons for not having a child (for instance, the pregnancy and birth were unexpected and interfered with their careers), and yet subconsciously they really wanted to have children. At birth these babies tended to be apathetic and lethargic.

These studies and others like them indicate how important it is for the mother to love and want to have her baby. If something is missing, then she—and, ideally, also her husband— should pray for a change in her attitude. For example, if she finds she is bearing an unplanned child, after the first surprise or shock at finding herself pregnant, it is important for her to try to develop a more positive attitude and welcome her child into her body and into the world. We don't know how the baby knows whether he is loved or rejected—or somewhere in between—but he does pick up on her feelings and somehow he will know.[6]

If her husband is not open to praying with her, then she can pray with a close woman friend, counselor or minister to ask Jesus to heal any attitude of hers that will hurt her baby. These negative attitudes may not be her fault at all; for instance, she may have been told by her mother that having children is very painful; or she herself may have suffered a miscarriage in a previous pregnancy. All of these memories naturally lead her to be fearful and anxious. If the anxiety is constant and becomes intense, adrenalin and all the hormones and enzymes that are activated by the mother's stress will steadily flow into the baby's body through the umbilical cord. The baby will share his mother's stress, even though he isn't able to understand its cause.

Dr. Monika Lukesch states that the *mother's attitude toward her unborn infant* is the single greatest influence on how the child will turn out, emotionally and physically. Loving, nurturing mothers generally give birth to secure, self-confident children, while unhappy, depressed, ambivalent mothers give birth to anxious, suspicious, emotionally fragile children.[7]

Next to the importance of the mother's attitude comes that of her husband. If he loves his wife and is faithful to her, he gives her a security that is vital to her pregnancy. On the other hand, Dr. Dennis Stott

> rates a bad marriage or relationship as among the greatest causes of emotional and physical damage in the womb. On the basis of a recent study of over thirteen hundred children and their families, he estimates a woman locked in a stormy marriage

runs a 237 percent greater risk of bearing a psychologically or physically damaged child than a
woman in a secure, nurturing relationship.[8]

What a wonderful, gentle revolution would be worked if
the meager number of Christian couples who pray together
would grow to millions of couples praying together twice a day
for their children waiting to be born. Their love for each other
would grow, and the unborn children would catch the overflow
of that love. So we encourage you to pray for the growth and
health of your child; pray that God's love may fill your baby
even now. Sing to your child; play beautiful music; talk to your
child. Know that your love will make a difference!

If you are ambivalent about having this child, try first to
work out your ambivalence by talking about it with your partner. See a Christian counselor if you need to. We know that,
unfortunately, many husbands and wives find it hard to share
together, to pray together. But, hopefully, even if you can't talk
openly with your husband, you will at least have a trustworthy
friend that you can share with.

One sobering and healthy effect of having children is that it
helps show us how much we tend to rely on material things
rather than upon God for our happiness. If our plans for promo-
tion, for a career, or buying a new house are interrupted by
pregnancy, it may provide us with a chance to change our
priorities and to learn to trust God. If your ambivalence about
having a baby flows from fears over which you have little control, then seek someone—ideally your spouse—and pray with
that person for your inner healing. Jesus can touch anything in
your past that takes away your freedom and your ability to live
in the present moment. This kind of prayer for yourself is separate, of course, from praying for the little child within you.

Ideally, to pray for your own inner healing, you and your
partner should choose a special time to set aside—a Saturday

afternoon, for example. Then share your thoughts, your hopes and your fears about the coming birth. Share those painful, negative feelings that might in any way stand in the way of a successful pregnancy. Then pray for one another to bless and affirm all the good, beautiful qualities you see in each other, and heal the negative attitudes that might harm your child. We often find it hard to share and to pray in depth because we really need to set a time, to "make an appointment," as it were, with our partner when we will be undisturbed; we let time go by and are absorbed by the immediate, such as jobs around the house that need to be taken care of, and we let the more important things go. A wise spiritual saying states that we are so attracted by the *urgent* that we never deal with what is truly *important.* We need to make time with Jesus for our marriage relationship to grow and to let him increase our love for the tiny infant within.

One special area where we may need to repent—to change our attitude—is when we so strongly desire to have a child of one sex that we reject the other. If we are disappointed to find that our newborn baby is a boy—or a girl—then our disappointment may permanently affect that little child. The father's preference, especially, is often for a boy. This can devastate the child later when it finds it is the "wrong" sex. We have talked with many people, including several close friends, who needed healing because of a lifelong sense of being unwanted because they were the wrong sex in the estimation of their father or mother. This puts the child in a desperate situation, because it cannot change its sex to please the parent; it is trapped in a sense of permanent rejection. So, be ready to welcome your child with delight, whether it turns out to be a boy or a girl. If we reject our baby because it's a son or a daughter, the problem lies not in the baby but in us; something in our attitude toward that unwanted sex needs to be healed.

A dramatic example of this was a woman whom Judith met

and counseled at a conference. This woman came to Judith because she had an infant son who was withering away and refused to take nourishment. The doctors could find nothing medically wrong with her baby and she was desperate about what to do. The woman's problem was compounded because this was the second time this had happened: her firstborn had also refused to eat. (He, too, had been a boy.) The doctors could find nothing wrong. And the infant had died. Now, here it was, happening all over again.

During a session of prayer and counsel, the mother told Judith that her father had abused her when she was a child, and she hated men. It became apparent that she hated having an infant son, who might grow up to be like her father and her husband—she didn't want to bring another man into the world. She admitted that she simply propped up the baby's bottle and refused to hold him. The child sensed his mother's rejection and, in turn, refused to take the bottle (a classic case of what doctors call "marasmus").

The story had a happy ending, for Judith asked the woman to forgive her father—which she did. Then Judith prayed, asking God the Father to come and be a father to her, supplying everything that was missing in her relationship with her earthly father. The woman had a powerful experience of God the Father's presence that healed her. As a result, her attitude toward her infant son totally changed. She started singing to her baby, holding him and cuddling him. Next thing, he started taking the bottle and putting on weight. And now she has a healthy son!

HEALING OF YOUR OWN PAST

In this book, we want to concentrate on the positive, on how wonderful it is for a mother and father to truly love God and each other and then to love the new life that comes out of their love union. Our earnest desire is to encourage couples to

pray with one another and for the newly conceived infant starting to grow within the mother.[9]

Yet, just as medical science has to take a good look at sickness, healing prayer also has to look at the negatives—the sin
and sickness—in us that need healing. Even now, in reading
what we have said so far, you may have become aware of areas
in your own inner life that need healing. If, as Dr. Lake states,
most of our serious psychological disorders begin as early as the
first three months in the womb, then we need the power of
Jesus to go back with us to the beginning and heal our own
deepest wounds. He believes that the afflictions of later life are
faithful reproductions of the crises first encountered in the earliest weeks of embryonic life and that any severe maternal
distress imprints itself upon the fetus.[10]

So bear with us as we share a little about the pain Dr. Lake
believes may touch the infant who suffers a mother's rejection
within those first three months. (The majority of us who have
not been afflicted with such pain should simply thank God that
we have been spared.) Lake calls this pain "Affliction" and says
that when such an afflicted person grows up he may be affected
physically; for instance, his stomach region may be tied up in
knots, his shoulders hunched. Sometimes this Affliction is at the
root of colitis. Often the person feels a pain near the navel,
which is felt to be a point of entry (as was the umbilical cord) for
the "black flood."[11]

In their inmost selves, afflicted people feel worthless; they
usually resist any help that is offered, and their death wish is
always strong. They feel a profound guilt at just existing. (Crimi-
nals usually do not feel as much guilt as some innocent people
do.) God is felt to be distant, or, worse yet, as condemning.
Sometimes the afflicted person is reflecting the self-condemna-
tion of his unmarried mother when she was made to feel de-
graded because she was raped or was forced into incest. Somehow the fetus picks up on this and turns its revulsion in on itself.

Later in life, he may turn his eyes away when people look at him, for he has a sense that "people can see my badness by looking into my eyes." Later, too, this self-hate can affect the skin (eczema)[12] or move into the sexual area which is felt as being evil. "Woe to the fetus whose lot is to spend forty weeks in such a desolate place," says Dr. Lake about the child growing in the womb of a mother who hates herself.[13]

We find it hard to write about such painful things; it is really only made bearable by the fact that Jesus can bring healing even to these most desolate situations. For those of us who only remember happiness and joy, in thinking of our own infancy and childhood, it is sobering to realize the depths of pain that some of our friends experience. The well-adjusted tend to say, "If these despondent friends would only straighten up and start to think about happy things and praise God, they would be all right." It is true, there are things we can make right by making a decision and sticking to it, with God's help. But the essence of sickness (such as alcoholism) is that we *can't do it* alone; we need God's help and healing. Those who are emotionally sick deeply experience St. Paul's dilemma: "I cannot understand my own behavior. I fail to carry out the things I want to do, and I find myself doing the very things I hate" *(Rm.* 7:15).

Most of us do need to exercise more self-discipline, but for the most deeply wounded areas of our lives, we need also to rely on the healing power of Jesus. Mrs. Agnes Sanford, a committed Christian and wife of a minister, had to endure seven years of mental depression before discovering how Jesus could heal her:

"These ways are precisely contrary to the usual suggestion infuriatingly given by those who know nothing. 'Come on, snap out of it,' they say. 'Be yourself!' Anything more asinine than this remark would be impossible to imagine. As if we could be ourselves merely by deciding to be ourselves! One cannot control the emotions of the deep mind simply by an act of will power. It is as stupid as saying to someone with two broken legs, 'Come now, snap out of it! A brisk walk around the block—that is what you need!' . . . The mental depressive is usually one who refrained from complaining; who has put himself under such long and rigid control that he is worn out from the effort. To suggest further effort is useless."[14]

Most of us, of course, are not as deeply wounded as the "Afflicted" whom Dr. Lake writes about, but if our mothers were severely depressed or anxious or were ambivalent about bringing another child into this world, we can still be affected, even though we are now thirty or forty years old. How can we pray to ask Jesus to free us from our depression or anxiety?

First, we should realize that there is no single set way of praying that will always work. Our healing lies in the power of Jesus, and not in some technique. Having said that, here are several suggestions (not rules) that you can follow in praying:

You can pray by yourself, but it does seem a help to ask someone to pray with you. We are usually so wrapped up in our own problems that we have trouble hearing the Lord in a positive way; we need to pray with someone who loves us and is sympathetic, but who can also be somewhat objective. Ideally, our husband or wife would be the one we would choose to pray with us. But for those who find it hard to pray with their partner, they can choose a close spiritual friend to pray with. If the wound is severe enough, a Christian counselor who believes in healing prayer (and there are an increasing number of them) would be an excellent—and sometimes necessary—help.

Whoever does the praying should really pray for guidance about *how* best to pray with you. You had best be in a quiet, comfortable place; crying often accompanies this kind of healing prayer, so it is good to be in a secluded place where you can cry if you need to. (You may need to give yourself permission to cry.) Then ask Jesus (or God the Father) to go back to that little infant who still lives within you and pray that Jesus will do whatever is necessary to heal those wounds. Most of the time, in my experience, the person sees, in the Spirit, Jesus touching or, better yet, holding that tiny being in his hand (something like that well-known sculpture of the little child cradled in the giant hand of God). You may feel the pains of the past draining out; gradually your tears will cease as the bitterness and rejection depart.[15] We found that it often helps for us to hold the person being healed in our arms (provided this can be done in a nonsexual context, as when a team or a couple ministers to the person, or when a husband prays with his wife). If you are not too sure about how best to pray for inner healing, you might read one of the fine books that have recently been published; they will give you some practical ideas on how you can pray for your inner child and be freed from the fears that have been with you from the very beginning.[16]

Often, as we pray, God somehow speaks directly to the person in words such as, "You are my beloved daughter, I love you and I will never desert you. I will take all your pain and change it to joy."

Here is a beautiful story about how the Lord healed one "ambivalent" mother and her son:

"Francis, you may remember praying for a child and his mother at the same time last night. That mother was me and that child was Joseph. Anyway, it never occurred to me for my children to be in the healing service—I thought it would scare them or they might be disruptive, etc. But, as soon as I saw children being prayed for, the Lord told me I had to go and get Joseph. I felt drawn by that one purpose as I ran up the rainy mountainside to the cabin where my husband was preparing him for bed. I fetched him and he never cried, wiggled or whimpered. He was so loving, so accepting, so trusting. Francis prayed for us and we both rested *together* in the Spirit.[17] That has to be from God!—What mother in her right mind would fall backwards with a forty-two-pound baby in her arms! He was so precious; he stirred before I did and said, 'Mommy, what are you sleeping on the floor for?'

"Joseph was my third child. He is only thirteen months younger than his brother Harry. I became pregnant while nursing and nurturing Harry so I found it very difficult to accept that another life inside me also needed nurturing. I was ambivalent about the pregnancy, and—yes—a little resentful, only because of the time element involved. I was very ill the entire nine months, and yet I had my other two children to love and provide for.

"I did grow to love and accept him as he grew within my womb, and I realized what a wonderful blessing he was when he was born.

"But that womb time is what the Lord chose to heal last night. He ministered to us both so that I know, beyond the shadow of a doubt, that Joseph won't have to deal with feelings of rejection at age thirty, since God healed him at age three! He truly reconciled us last night. I rocked him for hours and told him all the things you would like to tell your unborn baby. It was truly a *holy* time, led by the Lord![18]

Chapter Five

FREEDOM FROM
NEGATIVE FORCES

(by Francis)

We want our thoughts and prayers for our unborn child to be
filled with life, anticipation and joy. And yet spiritual realism
makes us recognize that occasionally during the pregnancy we
may need to pray so that our child may be freed from any
harmful spiritual forces that may have come down to him
through our ancestry. Many children will not need to be freed
from such harmful ancestral influences, but, in our experience,
there are also some who do. Perhaps the best time to pray for
this freedom (if you think it necessary) is during the first trimester, or shortly afterward; for if this isn't done early in our lives,

we may need to deal with these harmful influences later. (Recently I heard Derek Prince say that about one out of four adults that he prays with for healing also needs to be freed from a family curse, before the healing can take place.)

So, we want to share with you three possible problem areas in your ancestry that you may want to pray about at some particular point in the pregnancy—the earlier the better.

1) First, if your family has a *hereditary predisposition to fall sick* from any disease, whether physical or spiritual, you can pray that Jesus will free your child of this weakness. In my own ancestry, for instance, there has been a certain amount of alcoholism, so Judith and I have asked Jesus to break that bondage. If your family is prone to sickle-cell anemia, or to heart disease, why not pray for your child to be freed from that weakness at the very beginning of his life? In Judith's family, for example, there is a predisposition toward serious respiratory problems, so we needed to pray for our children to be preserved from this weakness.

The ideal kind of prayer to free your child is a prayer of command. You might, for instance, pray like this: "Jesus, you know my family has a predisposition to (here identify the weakness). We ask you to break this weakness and free our child, in your name. By the sword of the Spirit, let our child be set free from any weakness or inclination to (again, name the weakness)! Let our child be set free at any level this weakness exists, whether it be spiritual or physical. If there is any demonic force that influences this sickness, we bind up that evil force in your name. And now we command you, spirit of infirmity (or addiction), to leave our child and go straight to Jesus for him to deal with, as he will! And now, Lord Jesus, fill our child with your health, your love and your power to replace any weakness that may have been there. And we thank you, Lord Jesus, that this is being done."

2) The second negative force—and this one is spiritual and demonic—results when our relatives or ancestors have been involved in *spiritualism,* especially if any of them acted as a medium or practiced witchcraft. The descendants may not always be influenced by their ancestors' occult activities but we find that such spiritualistic involvement frequently does cause unhappiness and havoc in later generations. If you suspect that your family has been involved in spiritualism or witchcraft you should first renounce the involvement, and then pray to set your family and child free from any evil influence that may have descended from previous generations; you should also bind up and cast forth any spirit of the occult (or witchcraft) and then consecrate your child to God through Jesus Christ in the power and unity of the Holy Spirit. (Of course, if you know that your ancestors have been heavily involved in spiritualism or witchcraft, you should, first of all, receive prayer for your own freedom from these occult spirits.)[1] Judith, when she directed a house of prayer in Jerusalem, needed (to her surprise) nearly eight hours of prayer for deliverance by Pastor Ralph Van Koey; much of this was as a result of a harmful spiritual influence in her ancestry.

3) Beyond that, a few families have been *cursed* in some way or another. To most people (in the United States, at least) the possibility of a curse may seem straight out of the middle ages, but we still sometimes find a family or person who has fallen under a curse, especially in areas where witchcraft is prevalent. In most non-European cultures a belief in the power of curses is taken for granted; in Nigeria, for instance, many people approached me to ask if I would set them free from curses that had been directed their way by witch doctors. Yet, we also find the effects of curses here in our own country— usually dating back a generation or two—a curse directed at an entire family. When we pray for a person who truly has been

cursed and the curse is broken, the change for the better is often dramatic. When an entire family seems to be inflicted by "bad luck"—unexplainable sickness, suicides and serious accidents—you may suspect that such a family needs to be freed from some oppression or curse.[2]

If you do suspect that anything like this has happened to your family, you would do well to ask someone with spiritual authority (e.g., a priest or minister who believes in the possibility of such cursing) to pray for you and your unborn child. If you don't know of any such minister, then pray as a couple for Jesus to free you, your family and your unborn child from any harmful ancestral influences.[3]

If you are not sure that any deliverance or freeing prayer is necessary, you can always say a *conditional* prayer: "*If* anyone in our family has been involved in spiritualism, I cut my child free of this influence . . ."

These precautionary prayers usually need only be said *once;* your prayers immediately following the time of conception should basically be positive, happy and filled with hope. Most couples won't need any of these prayers to free their child from harmful ancestral influences. They can pray without anxiety, in joy, thanking God for the beauty of creation and the miracle of life that is silently growing within the mother's womb.

Chapter Six

THE SECOND TRIMESTER

(*by Francis*)

By praying during the fourth to sixth months of your pregnancy you are simply continuing what you began so beautifully three months ago. But there are two additional special purposes of prayer we want to talk about at this time:

1) The overcoming of *depression,* and of

2) unnecessary *stress* and *anxiety* in your life.

For both depression and anxiety prayer is a powerful antidote. But, above all, a mother's love is the single most powerful protection her child can have against depression, as well as against undue stress.[1] What matters most is not any external stress you may be experiencing in your life, but how you feel about having your child. The best protection your child can have—because even now he can pick up on your stress—is if you deeply desire to have this child; the greatest stress both you and your child can experience is if you reject your pregnancy and your child. This is mainly true of the mother, but it is true of the father as well. The love and acceptance of life by both mother and father will be the best guarantee that their baby will love life and, in turn, will feel loved.

Over and above the mother's love for her child, like an outer layer of protection, the husband's love surrounds his wife and the child lying within her. The mother enfolds her child not only with the warmth of her body but with the warmth of her love. And she, in turn, is enfolded by the loving arms of her husband. This is beautifully symbolized when the husband and his wife are praying together for one another and for their child.

Already your baby's personality is being formed: it is being disposed toward openness, toward self-confidence and an openness to people and to life. Most of all, the child is being blessed by God, the creator of goodness and life. During the second trimester your little child's consciousness is first beginning to stir; by the sixth month, your child will be able to make subtle discriminations about your feelings and attitudes.[2] In a special way, your love—or your rejection—can affect your child at this very early age. Your child will sense your love and acceptance and will respond to them by growing peacefully within the security of your womb. As a Christian it is encouraging for you to realize that your own experience of love, joy and peace (the primary fruits of the Holy Spirit) can also touch your child with a corresponding love, joy and peace.

Nobody knows for sure how such a tiny infant can pick up on your feelings. Is it simply because the hormones your body secretes when you are happy—or depressed or anxious—travel

through the umbilical cord and cause the fetus to respond physically, or is it for some other mysterious reason (perhaps your
child's spirit is somehow listening and responding to you)? We
simply don't know, but since there is so much evidence that the
unborn child at this stage does respond to your feelings, positive
and negative, you need to provide a positive emotional environment just as you try to provide the best physical environment
by caring for your diet and by avoiding smoking and excessive
drinking. It's just as important, perhaps more so.

A mother cannot, certainly, avoid all sadness and stress.
Emotions are normal aspects of life and are God-given helps to
motivate you to act. But when sadness lengthens into depression and momentary tension builds into constant anxiety, then
these feelings may harm your child.

DEPRESSION

That constant sadness we call depression weakens everything we do and spreads its gloom over our lives. The sun is
darkened and the clouds never seem to lift. Eventually, we
don't feel like doing anything except sleep. Agnes Sanford, in
her classic *Healing Gifts of the Spirit*,[3] describes how she endured a deep depression for seven years and how Jesus lifted it
through prayer. If the pregnant mother is prone to depression
this can affect her child; in fact, treating infant depression has
become one of psychiatry's main priorities.[4] As you know, this
predisposition to melancholy can be deepened by the mood
swings so common in pregnancy, due to the hormonal changes
going on in the mother's body. So, some mothers are physiologi-
cally predisposed to fall prey to depression.

From outside, one of the main causes of depression is suffering a major *loss*. For example, if a pregnant mother's father or
mother should die, or if her husband should lose his job, this
kind of loss can easily precipitate a depression that can affect

her pregnancy. Once she becomes aware of this, however, she can pinpoint the cause of her sadness and then

1) share her feelings with someone she trusts, and

2) pray, asking Jesus to totally heal the depression,

or else to help her by carrying her cross with her so that she will not be alone in bearing her sorrow. When a mother does experience a great loss—such as a death or a divorce—she naturally tends to withdraw into herself; in doing this she also tends to withdraw some of her love for her child; she is distracted. The long-term effect of her loss, of her depression, may be that her baby is also affected by a kind of listlessness, or apathy—the same way a depressed adult is affected.

STRESS AND ANXIETY

In a similar way, the mother's undue anxiety can invade her infant; if her anxiety is excessive her baby may later turn out to be colicky, suffer from gastric problems, be hyperactive and underweight. Stress is a normal part of life and will only harm the child if it lasts for a *long time* and touches the mother in a very *personal* way. Apparently we are able to withstand a great deal of environmental stress, but when there is a breakdown in relationships with those we love, that is when stress can be most damaging. Dr. Verny, for example, quotes a Finnish study which indicates that psychiatric disorders that occur later in life, especially schizophrenia, are more frequent among those persons whose fathers had died before they were born. In some mysterious way, the extreme distress these mothers experienced when their husbands died seems to have touched their babies. It is truly amazing how all this happens. Love and peace beget more love and peace. Anxiety breeds anxiety, and hate leads to hate. I once prayed for a woman for deliverance from a spirit that called itself "Hatred of Men." The woman's mother had been a prostitute, who, as a result, hated men with such fury that she came to be influenced by an evil force which, in turn, was passed on to her daughter. Apparently this transmission of a hateful spirit happened before birth. When Jesus put his emphasis on our forgiving those who injure us, he was reversing our human spiral of hate that has plagued our history from the very beginning.

A remarkable example of how a mother's stress may influence children later in life is given by Dr. Frank Lake:

"Mothers can be encouraged to take as much care to be at peace with themselves in the nine months before the birth as in the nine months of concentrated nursing after it . . . I was speaking some time ago to a group that included an American mother of three daughters. She returned to me excitedly a few hours later, saying that what I had said explained for the first time the behavior of the middle daughter. What made it significant was that a number of other girls in the same class were behaving in almost exactly the same way. They had manifested an unaccountable tendency to break down suddenly into crying and sobbing. They were not just sad, but deeply distressed with a cutting sense of shame and guilt that some terrible thing had happened. What it was they were devastated by, or why they did it, neither they nor their parents had any idea. Her elder daughter and her classmates in the form above had no such tendency, nor had the daughter lower down in the school and her friends. They had wondered about an hysterical group phenomenon, but it was most unlike such outbreaks. The illumination that had come to her she expressed by saying, 'I have just realized that that was exactly my behavior in 1963, when my daughter was early on in my womb, as the other girls would be in their mothers', when J. F. Kennedy was shot. That was exactly my behavior. For weeks, we were prone to breaking into

tears with just those feelings about the shooting of the President. The whole thing makes sense to me for the first time.' "[6]

A single example like this proves little scientifically, but it
certainly fits the evidence we have gathered in our years of
praying with people; it is simply amazing how God has con-
structed the human spirit in such a delicate way and how sensitive we are to the influence of other people—for good or for
evil. Little wonder that Jesus' great commandment was that we
should love one another—especially little children.

An extraordinary example of this sensitivity to stress occurs
when a fetus apparently becomes aware that its life is in danger
from abortion. We will say more about this in the appendix on
miscarriage and abortion, but here we will simply pass on Dr.
Lake's observation that he believes that at eleven weeks the
fetus already knows when it is in danger.

By eleven weeks, with the completion of the basic genesis
of organs, the fetus, as we know from the reliving of attempted
or failed abortions at that time, knows that its presence is re-
sented and its life is in danger. It relives its own near-murder
with quite shocking accuracy and overwhelming terror.[7]

Again, psychiatrist Thomas Verny made a study of his own
patients and found that 66 percent said that their mothers suffered from a great deal of stress during the time of pregnancy.[8]

Our conclusions from all this: that mothers should follow
the ancient custom of Jewish mothers by taking special care to
avoid unnecessary anxiety and stress. The husband can greatly
help in this by affirming and loving his wife, and by supporting
her during the mood swings and nausea that may affect her.
Clearly he needs to be faithful at all times, but especially so now.

In spite of all the care we take, we find that our human
situation is frail and there may be tragedies and stresses in our

lives that we cannot avoid. Your mother discovers she has cancer, your closest friend discovers her husband is unfaithful, your husband is severely injured in an accident—or the President is unexpectedly and tragically shot to death. All of this is part of life and we cannot escape it. But you, as a Christian, have a very special help in the healing love of Jesus. In the first place you can pray for protection; I firmly believe that several times our family has been preserved from accidents simply because we pray every morning to be surrounded by God's protective shield. But if tragedy has already struck, you can pray to be healed from the stress or sadness that has overwhelmed you so that it will become bearable and not touch your child. Do not let sadness grow into a continual depression or stress build up into a lasting anxiety.

Again, we encourage the mother to pray for, as well as to talk and sing to, her unborn child, just as she will a few months from now when her baby lies nestled in her arms. She can flood her child with love, and welcome him into this world (which right now is confined to that small space below her heart).

If the husband can join his wife in prayer several times a day it will be ideal. If something should go wrong, if she finds herself severely depressed or stressed, she can ask her husband or a close friend to pray with her, asking Jesus to free her from any excessive sadness or fear.

Perhaps, as you read this chapter, you suspect that a general sadness that has always pervaded your life goes back to a loss that your mother suffered when she was carrying you. Or you recognize that the restless anxiety that agitates you has its roots in some severe stress that tormented your mother when she carried you. If so, you can be freed from that depression or from that anxiety. Go to a minister or friend, whom you know to be sensitive to the Holy Spirit, and ask him to pray with you for a healing of that little child who is still crying within you, waiting to be lifted up and consoled.[9]

If you have no particular friend to pray with, then you can go to Jesus himself. Try to listen for any inspirations he may send you as to how you can best pray for yourself. We find that most healing prayers for this early time of our lives have a connection with touch, since touch, rather than words, is the way love is usually communicated to a child. Often Jesus simply seems to appear; he takes and holds the crying child in his arms until the sobbing dies down and turns into a deep peace.

You can pray very simply. For instance, you can start by putting yourself in the presence of Jesus. See him as best you can in your imagination; talk to him. I am constantly surprised at how often he actually seems to come to the person in a very *real* way. We ourselves cannot make this happen. It is pure gift. But it does happen from time to time that Jesus, as it were, takes over the prayer. If this should happen to you, be grateful; you should be healed (even of lifetime ailments) whenever Jesus himself directs the time of prayer.

But if you are the one saying the prayer, or picturing Jesus in your imagination, you can then ask him to journey back with you to the time when you were still in your mother's womb. Ask him to heal you and your mother of the sadness and fear that touched you both. I often feel guided in prayer to ask Jesus to touch that tiny unborn child, to hold it in his hands until all fear and anxiety drain away. There are many ways you can pray, so try to follow the spirit so that your prayer will be specially tailored to your own situation. The following is an example of how God can take over and direct a prayer for healing. It happened when I was praying for a mother who was adopted; she felt so rejected that she could not believe that God loved her. Part of her problem was demonic, so we prayed to free her from those evil forces that had oppressed her all her life. Here is what happened next:

"Right in front of me appeared the Manger Scene. I could not see the baby Jesus—he was but a bright light in the crib—but I could see Mary and Joseph adoring him. Then it faded and Mary appeared. She reached her arms out to me and took me to herself as a baby. She held me and loved me. Then the light that was in Jesus flooded me . . . I felt new life, as if it were a new birth. I was new! I was healed! I was overwhelmed with a love for God, my Father.

"The next thing I saw was what looked like a golden gate that raised up in front of me. Then the demons tried lunging to reenter my body, but they could not get past this gate.

"I then broke down and cried—a depth-rending cry—and I felt at last at peace with God.

"My life *has* changed."

Just as he freed this mother, so deeply fearful because of a wounding that happened way back in her mother's womb, so Jesus can free you.

> For this is what the Lord says:
> "I will extend peace to her like a river,
> and the wealth of nations like a flooding stream;
> you will nurse and be carried on her arm
> and dandled on her knees.
> As a mother comforts her child,
> so will I comfort you" *(Is.* 66:12–13, NIV).

Chapter Seven

THE THIRD TRIMESTER

(by Judith)

By the time you reach the seventh month, it will be obvious to you that your baby is a sensitive, alert and responsive being. You have felt the kicks, the quiet sleeping periods and the very active moments. The fetus, while growing physically, is also developing mentally and emotionally. The "Blank Tablet" theory (which declares that we enter the world like a blank slate) was held for many years by some scientists, but has, in recent years, been challenged. They now believe that the intrauterine environment does help shape the person we become in many significant ways. Until recently, it was very difficult to find researchers interested enough to study this new field. Now, a growing number of practitioners are committing their expertise to studying perinatal psychology. Proponents of perinatal psychology see birth as a continuum of physical and psychological events, beginning with conception and continuing through postnatal bonding. Many of their findings support a growing awareness that the baby is consciously aware of her environment, both physically and emotionally, especially during the last trimester. Studies indicate that, at twenty-eight weeks in utero, the baby displays coordinated states of consciousness such as waking, sleeping and dreaming. Your baby's ears are functional at this time, leading us to assume that she is beginning to learn. Your baby can not only hear the swooshing blood in your vessels, your breathing and your rhythmic heartbeat, but she can also hear your voice, and more faintly, the voice of her daddy. Joan Lunden, host of ABC's "Good Morning America," shared this about her experiences with her unborn daughter:

> We didn't read or play special music while she was in the womb, but every night my husband, Michael, would talk to my tummy. He'd say "Hello there, this is your father speaking," and then he'd sing a musical scale. He always did the same thing. When Jamie was born, she cried endlessly. Then Michael held her. He said, "Hello, this is your father speaking." And he sang the scale. The baby looked up at him and stopped crying.[1]

Other controlled studies of fetal learning indicate that the baby has a *strong* preference for the mother's voice at birth, and also prefers the same stories that were read to her during her time in utero.

One sign of the times is that Dr. F. Rene Van de Carr has

started a unique Prenatal University in Hayward, California, where he teaches expectant parents to communicate with their unborn children. Van de Carr believes in channeling the baby's perceptions at five months with the "kick game," a way of getting the child's attention twice a day. When the baby kicks, the parent pats that spot, then waits for the baby to kick again. " 'After you don't do anything for a minute or two,' Van de Carr said, 'the baby kicks again. You pat again, then pause. The baby waits for a little while, then kicks again. If you pat someplace else, the baby may actually move its foot to kick where you patted.' "[2] After two months of the kick game, the baby's response pattern is established, and Van de Carr adds his primary word list, six basic words connected with distinct physical sensations: pat, rub, squeeze, shake, stroke and tap. He also has the parents begin talking to the baby and playing music—the same soothing song each time. One study involving 150 mothers of the Prenatal University program, showed that these babies had a significantly higher incidence of pre-speech, early speech, and use of compound words.[3] These mothers also reported that their children were less fearful, more attentive, quick and adaptable. In a separate follow-up study of five hundred babies born after their parents took the program at Prenatal University, the researchers found "enhanced physical and mental development, including easy birth, early speech, physical agility, and healthy parent-child bonding."[4]

Another program for prenatal learning is the Susedik Method, developed by Joseph and Jitsuko Susedik. When Joseph was five years old, his Polish grandmother told him it was a Polish custom for pregnant women to rock their unborn babies and sing them stories about the family history to prepare them for life. When the Susediks had their own four daughters, they began teaching each of them, beginning at five months in utero, and then continued the lessons after they were born. "The oldest daughter, Susan, fourteen, a high school freshman at age five," wrote John Grossman, "is now a senior in college. Her I.Q. has been tested at over 235. Her three sisters all have I.Q.s over 150."[5]

How this learning occurs is being clarified through modern techniques designed to study the unborn child. According to Dr. Verny, "Dr. Dominick Purpura, editor of the journal *Brain Research*, Professor at Albert Einstein Medical College, and head of the study section on the brain of the National Institutes of Health, puts the start of awareness between the twenty-eighth and thirty-second week. By this point, he notes, the brain's neural circuits are just as advanced as a newborn's."[6]

Dr. Verny states that the fact that the unborn child has proven abilities to react to her surroundings through her senses shows that she has the basic prerequisites for learning.[7]

The point being made by these researchers is that your unborn baby is very much involved in her life, limited though it is, and though researchers argue about the exact time this awareness begins, they are all in agreement that your baby does feel, respond and learn. Whatever way you choose to relate to your baby is just that—your choice. But it is important for you to decide to interact with your baby and allow her to know that she is loved and wanted.

INTRAUTERINE BONDING

Your affirmation of this new, developing life is essential for the well-being of your baby. The opposite of affirmation, a sense of rejection, can be sensed by your baby and will create difficulties, both before and after birth. Just to give you a personal example, a young man, whom we will call Peter, came to me for help in my private practice. He was in his mid-twenties and had experienced difficulties in his perception of himself since his seventeenth year. He was a very sensitive, gentle and intelligent young man, and a deeply committed Christian. From all outward appearances he seemed to be doing well, but inside he was deeply troubled. So many people are like this, good people who lead good lives, but are haunted within by feelings of rejection due to their early experiences. As our sessions progressed, it became obvious that Peter's inner sense of rejection, though concealed until he was seventeen, dated back to the earliest moments of his life. As we prayed together, the Lord seemed to direct us to pray concerning the time right before Peter's birth. As I led the prayer, and asked Jesus to surround Peter with his love in the womb, he suddenly, and quite unexpectedly, said, "I'm not going to come out! I don't want to be born—they don't want me." He became distressed and fearful, and the fear related to life itself. His memory of not being wanted by his parents had been brought to the surface by the Holy Spirit, and the Lord was healing the pain of that memory. Peter's parents were older, with their other children nearly grown, and his mother's pregnancy came as an unwanted surprise. Though very good people, they were not prepared emotionally and they did not want a new baby. This rejection was picked up by Peter, even in the womb, and made him afraid to be born. An unborn child is not affected by mild stress in the mother, but intense or prolonged stress can be dangerous. The anxiety and stress-related hormones pass through the umbilical cord into the unborn child's bloodstream, along with a sense of being unwanted. This combination of negatives, both physical and psychological, is too much for the baby to cope with. In Peter's case, his mother's meager love was not enough to give him a strong sense of self, or a desire to live. As a result, later in life, the fear and insecurities of those early experiences exploded into paranoia.

I have, over the years, prayed with several people like Peter. Their problems stem from a lack of bonding in utero. Just as positive, loving, life-giving feelings can be communicated to the baby, negative feelings can also be absorbed. The mother's emotions during pregnancy have both an immediate and a long-term influence on the child.

An extraordinary case of the effect of maternal stress was reported in *Psychology Today:*

"A healthy seventeen year old gave birth to an apparently normal baby after a medically uncomplicated pregnancy. Twenty-four hours of normal infant care followed, with mother and child side-by-side. Then the baby vomited fresh blood. He was examined and still appeared to be healthy, but his vomiting continued, and one hour later he died. Postmortem examination revealed three peptic ulcers. Since peptic ulcers usually develop in adults who are chronically tense and anxious, the physicians wondered whether the mother could have been under enough stress to pass ulcer-causing hormones across the placenta. In fact, her pregnancy, especially in the last trimester, was extraordinarily stressful. Coerced by her parents into marrying the father of her child, she found herself living with an alcoholic wife-batterer. . . . A single case certainly does not prove that maternal stress can cause gastric ulcers in a newborn, but the possibility does warrant some kind of counseling for pregnant women who are exceptionally tense, anxious or unhappy."[8]

This is an extreme example of intense maternal stress which had a tragic ending for the baby and his mother. Nevertheless, it is important to remember that not *all* stress means that the baby will be malformed or psychologically wounded. Some stress in our lives is unavoidable, and it can have a positive effect on the baby by providing stimuli to her brain. I think most of us would agree that we perform better under a certain amount of stress. Absolutely no pregnancy will be entirely stress-free, and we will exhaust ourselves if we try to control every aspect of our environment or our thinking. Stress, complications and fears should be met as a challenge by you, and God can help you handle it if you pray. There will not be many other times in your life when you will feel as "out of control" as you will during pregnancy. Prayer helps to bring you and your little one under the protection and care of the one who is the Creator of Life.

We learned, during both our pregnancies, to rely on our Lord and to trust his ability to bring his life and peace to our little one, even in the midst of difficulties.

When I was pregnant with David, our second-born, I was involved in a traffic accident. I was in my eighth month and definitely looked very pregnant. I had been on a shopping afternoon with two of my friends, and while driving home, we were struck from behind by another car. No one was seriously injured, but David became very distressed within me, and began kicking rapidly. When the emergency squad arrived, they took one look at me and decided I should go directly to the hospital, because they feared the accident might induce premature labor. I insisted that, instead of going to the hospital, my friends drive me home. Somehow I knew that if I could get home and pray with Francis, David would be fine. It took fifteen minutes for my friends to drive me home, and we prayed on the way, while David was kicking constantly. When I arrived home, I told Francis about the accident; he asked me to lie down and began praying immediately. Placing our hands over David, we asked our Lord to remove any fear from him as a result of the accident, and to fill him with peace, the peace of Jesus. Then we prayed that he be able to rest. He immediately became very still, all kicking ceased and he fell into a deep, peaceful sleep. Then Francis prayed for me, and a deep, calming peace filled my mind and body, and I slept along with David. After a wonderful, restful nap, I woke up feeling renewed. Today, there is not a trace of that fear or any adverse effects of that threatening accident in our son's life. The Lord completely healed the stress and trauma for both of us.

Perhaps you find yourself in a pregnancy which has been complicated by painful relationships, financial difficulties or physical problems. These stresses can affect you very deeply, and rob you of the joy of fully bonding with your baby. Sharing these concerns and fears with your husband, doctor or pastor should help release the stress which accompanies them, and prayer will place them where they belong—in the hands of God.

One of the questions which our pediatrician asked when she discovered the topic of this book was, "When does a mother's love for her baby begin?" For me, the answer seemed simple—it began the first moment I became aware a new life was growing within me—a life given by God in response to the love my husband and I have for each other. An astonishing miracle, the continuation of our life, our faith and our love, she was separate, but forever part of us. I felt a deep, protective, loving response to this wonderful little baby. It was immediate, yet grew even as my body grew. This intrauterine bonding, as I later learned it was called, was a natural flow of God's love, my husband's love and my love flowing to the child within. In the last trimester, the bonding increased as I felt my baby's increased movement. I wanted to comfort our baby, sing to her, talk to her and pray for her. It gave us great joy to pray for her, and to know that our prayer would fill her with God's love and protection. We've seen many mothers rub their tummies in an attempt to sooth and comfort the child within. Several mothers have told us how they enjoy talking or singing to their baby. All of this promotes intrauterine bonding—something women have naturally and instinctively done for ages. Thus, the bonding immediately following birth should be a natural continuation of what has been happening all along, especially in the last trimester when the child is so active.

One of our good friends, Jan Orth, was talking with me and I was sharing with her how children, until they are about three, can often remember being in the womb. So she later asked her son, Matthew (who was then about three), "Do you remember what it was like to be in mummy's tummy?" He started to giggle and the giggle grew into a deep belly laugh: "Oh, sure I remember! I remember I used to tickle you all the time with my foot." Then Jan recalled that when she was carrying him, Matthew's foot would seem to get stuck under her rib cage, causing her discomfort. He'd wiggle his foot, poking and tickling her. So Jan would push the foot back into place; ten minutes later he would have it back under her ribs, poking away. When this all happened, Jan had no idea her baby was playing. But here was Matthew laughing away and telling her that he "had fun tickling mommy."

Matthew was bonding with his mother, even though she didn't know it.

"IN PEACE I WILL BOTH LIE DOWN AND SLEEP"
(PS. 4:8)

The last trimester can be especially hard on you because of your chronic feelings of tiredness caused by changes in your body chemistry, and because of your carrying the combined weight of a fluid-filled womb and an active baby. Most of my time, especially during the last month of gestation, was spent trying to find ways to rest. This was not always easy, due to our schedule, and (when I was carrying David) trying to keep up with Rachel, a very active twenty-month-old. Rest is very important throughout your pregnancy, but is especially necessary during the time before birth. Your strength will be needed for the birth experience, and for a quick recovery following birth. Naps need to be routinely scheduled into your day. For our first pregnancy this was easy, as I was home alone. During our second pregnancy, I took naps with Rachel, since she was still taking two naps a day. If you have older children beyond the age of naps, perhaps you can make an arrangement for a quiet time in the house. When Francis was a young child, his mother insisted that he and his sister go to their rooms for a rest period. If they didn't want to sleep, they could read or play quietly. As a child, he couldn't understand why he needed this rest time—as a parent himself now, he understands why his mother needed it. We carry this tradition on in our family, as did Francis's sister with her four children.

Some women feel guilty if they rest or nap during the day, especially if they somewhat neglect cleaning house. Perhaps your mother had thirteen children, as my paternal grandmother did, and she never stopped working or thought of her own needs. The models you had of mother in your early life will affect you a great deal as you find your own way to becoming a mother. Few mothers take the necessary time to rest, pray or just have time alone. Your pregnancy is a good time to establish these rest habits, and to realize that you need them to maintain your strength and health. How to find rest is a good topic for you to discuss and plan with your husband. Francis and I try to help each other have rest times and alone times. If guilt plagues you when you treat yourself to a quiet time or rest, have your husband pray with you to be free of that irrational feeling—it has a root somewhere in you; discussing it and praying about it will help free you from false guilt. Remember, you and your emotional well-being are very valuable to your unborn baby and to the rest of your family.

Just at the time when you need rest the most, it often seems almost impossible to sleep. The sheer excitement of the miracle of birth is almost overwhelming. You are looking forward to finally *seeing* your precious baby, and holding her in your arms. This alone is enough to keep you awake. Then again, other concerns creep into your mind—do we have everything we need for the baby's homecoming? What will the birth experience be like? Will we make it to the hospital on time? I don't think I've ever slept the night before a vacation, much less before giving birth. When my labor began with Rachel, it was 3 A.M., and I woke up immediately. Then I waited a few minutes before waking Francis up. He timed the contractions and called the doctor. The doctor said it would be all right to stay at home until 7 A.M. and then come to the hospital. Francis told me I needed my rest so I should go back to sleep. He returned to bed, ready to try and sleep some more. But how does one "go back to sleep" when labor has begun for your firstborn? Maybe, when you have been through this several times, it is possible, I don't know, but I do know I could not go back to sleep that night— and neither did he. So we spent the next four hours sharing and praying.

Sleeping at night also becomes increasingly difficult during the last month of your pregnancy because your uterus has grown so big. It becomes almost impossible to find a comfortable position, short of sleeping standing up. Sleeping on your stomach is definitely out, a luxury you had to forfeit months ago. I have never been able to sleep on my back, so that, too, was ruled out. I also found that when I rested on my back for too long a period, the baby's weight pressed on certain vessels and affected my circulation, which resulted in dizziness. So, I was left with two positions—left side or right side. I could get a comfortable position on my side by gathering several pillows and tucking them under strategic points of my body and between my knees. After much effort, I could achieve a state of relative comfort, but not for long. During these weeks, we prayed and asked the Lord to renew my strength, as well as the strength of the little one inside me. We shared Scriptures filled with promises of rest and health, such as

I lie down and sleep;
I wake again, for the Lord sustains me *(Ps.* 3:5).
In peace I will both lie down and sleep;
for thou alone, O Lord,
makest me dwell in safety *(Ps.* 4:8).

"HE TOOK WITH HIM MARY, HIS FIANCÉE, WHO WAS OBVIOUSLY PREGNANT BY THIS TIME" (LK. 2:5, LB)

During my pregnancies, I thought often of Mary and the hardships she endured to bring Jesus into this world. The thought of her riding a donkey from Nazareth to Bethlehem during the week before birth was not a happy one. Having lived in Israel, I know the hardship which the land and climate offered Mary and Joseph as they traveled. The fact that she had no place to birth her baby was stressful, and must have been especially embarrassing for Joseph, whom God had appointed to care for her. Yet, the Scriptures tell us that Mary pondered all these things and kept them in her heart. She cherished all of her experiences during her pregnancy and following Jesus' birth.

Many women have difficulty accepting their growing shape. For some, it is a source of joy and pride, for others, of shame and embarrassment. I believe much of the latter has to do with our society's emphasis on beauty and thinness. Thin is in, and anyone with an extra ounce of fat is out. Remember the part in *Gone With the Wind* when Scarlett O'Hara was trying to get her waist cinched to 17 inches again after the birth of her daughter? It would only compress to 20 inches, and her maid told her it would never be 17 again because she had "done had a baby." Scarlett's response was "I'll take care of that; I'll never have another baby." Like Scarlett, some women have difficulty coping with their growing shape during pregnancy and their increased size after the baby is born. It's sad, a poor reflection on our values, when women feel this way. In other cultures, pregnant women display their stomachs with great pride. It's only in Western cultures, like our own, that pregnancy is hidden and not discussed. In the nineteenth century, it was only referred to as "her condition." This attitude is changing slowly, but, for some, pregnancy is still embarrassing. One friend told me I would eventually want to destroy all of the pictures taken of me during the last months of pregnancy. Yet, those are the photos I cherish the most, along with those of the birth itself, and our children love seeing the ones when "they were inside mommy's tummy." It gives them great joy to look at them.

When Rachel was three years old, she saw a man with a very large stomach, and she asked me, "Do all fat tummies have babies inside?" Unfortunately, many people associate fat with pregnancy. For some, early memories of rejection for being fat prevent their enjoying their body's growth to accommodate the baby. During both of our pregnancies, I gained forty pounds, and felt beautiful. I loved the growing evidence in my body of a big, healthy baby. I took care to eat properly and exercise regularly, so I knew my gain was healthy in proportion to the large babies I carried. I started wearing maternity clothes in the third month, not because I needed them, but because I wanted everyone to know and share in our joy. I was glad and thankful about my growing shape.

This joyful attitude was made possible by my loving husband's affirmation of the life we helped create, and also because the Lord had healed me of some of my childhood memories. My weight had always been a source of anxiety for me. As a child in elementary school, I was very overweight—at a time when it is critical for a girl to be accepted by her peer group. I suffered greatly because of the cruel remarks directed at me by fellow students. I saw the other girls who were thin making friends and getting all the invitations to go to parties. The mistaken belief grew within me that if I could only be thin, I would be liked and accepted. During junior high school, I started to diet and managed to lose pounds until I fell well below a healthy weight. Then I was too thin, and yet I still *felt* fat. The acceptance I had dreamed of came very easily, and I quickly moved into the right circles and became very popular. Yet, deep within me was locked the image of a young, fat, unpopular girl.

This image lived with me for twenty years. It wasn't until I attended a healing conference (given by Francis in Staten Island, N.Y.) that the Lord began to release those painful memories, long suppressed in the subconscious. During the healing service in the chapel, Francis asked the Holy Spirit to reveal to each one there something in their hearts that needed to receive the healing love of Jesus. I was completely surprised when a very painful memory, long forgotten, came unexpectedly to mind. The incident had happened on Valentine's Day when I was in third grade; the beautiful valentine I had made for a popular boy in the class was discovered by my teacher as it was passed across the classroom to a friend. As punishment, the teacher forced me to read it to the class. She and the class ridiculed me; it was yet another rejection. That evening in chapel, the Lord reminded me I had never forgiven the teacher and those children for hurting me. As my prayer partner prayed for me, I forgave each one who came to mind, and I asked the Lord to forgive me for the bitterness I had held in my heart against them.

A freedom came to me that night that has remained with me to this day. The fat girl that had been locked in my mind was released and healed, and integrated into my total self. My distorted body image was corrected, and the anxiety I had always lived with about my weight disappeared. For the first time in my life, I felt good about my body and accepted myself. Without that healing, I would never have been able to fully enter into the wonderful changes that happened to my body during pregnancy. (Incidentally within a few weeks—without dieting—I lost five pounds, and, aside from my pregnancies, it has never come back!) I have a deep reverence for my body now, and an acceptance of the way it was created. A wonderful sense of awe and thanksgiving dwells within me when I think of the wonder of my body bringing forth new life, and nourishing that new life through nursing.

God has created mothers to be partners with Him in bringing new human beings into His world, and so He provides your body and your spirit with everything your little one will need to grow and mature. It truly is a miracle, and you are part of it! If there is anything in your past (or present) that prevents you from accepting your role in this miracle, talk with your husband or friend about it, and pray to be set free. Maybe it is a memory such as mine, long since forgotten, but still affecting the way you feel about yourself or life. The Good News of the Kingdom is that as God's children we do not have to live with broken hearts or distorted self-images—He has come to make all things new!

> The Spirit of the Lord God is upon me,
> because the Lord has annointed me
> to bring good tidings to the afflicted;
> He has sent me to bind up the brokenhearted,
> to proclaim liberty to captives,
> and the opening of prison
> to those who are bound *(Is.* 61:1).

"YOU SHALL CALL HIS NAME JESUS." (LK. 1:31)

Perhaps by now you have already selected the name for your baby. If not, we would like to encourage you to pray and ask the Lord what name he has for your child. Selecting a name was very important in biblical times. In some ways it was believed that the name would reflect the destiny or character of the child. You will see this everywhere as you read the Scriptures. In numerous passages, God gives a name to the parents before the birth of the child, or else He changes the name of an adult to suit the mission to which He calls him. In Isaiah, we read: "The Lord called me from the womb, from the body of my mother he named my name" (49:1).

In telling Mary to name her baby "Jesus," Gabriel is also announcing to Mary his ministry, destiny and nature. Since, in ancient times, the name was closely related to the nature of its bearer, we already have a powerful description of the ministry of our Lord, even before he was born, for the name Jesus means "God saves," or "God heals." Every time we say the name "Jesus," we are also affirming our belief in his healing, saving ministry. Gabriel also appeared to Zechariah, as he was praying in the temple, and told him that Elizabeth would bear a son and that they should call him "John"—which means "God is gracious."

In some instances, God has changed the name of an adult to a name more suited to the character and calling of that person. Such was the case of Simon the apostle. Jesus changed his name to Peter, or Cephas, meaning "rock." This indicated more accurately Peter's character and destiny ("On this rock I will build my community" *Mt*. 16:18, NJB). I have some friends who changed their names legally as adults, because they didn't feel their own name fit. In naming your baby, you may not have an angel appear to you with her name, and a proclamation of her destiny, but if you pray, you will receive an intimation, an inner sense about the right name for your child. This was the way it happened with both of our babies; after prayer, one name emerged from all the rest, and—it is true—their names seem to reflect our childrens' characters.

I believe my name "Judith" was given to my mother in

prayer, as I have always felt it suited my mission in life. It means "Jewess." When I moved to Israel in the mid-seventies, that name took on a new meaning. I had felt called to Israel for several years and responded to that call, not knowing what was in store for me. When I arrived in Jerusalem, I finally understood what had been obscurely felt in my heart for years. I immediately felt at home with the land and the people, and experienced a deep peace, even though I was in a country torn by war and terrorist attacks. I knew I was in the center of God's perfect will, and found it easy to love and the work He had called me to. I was so happy!

As a Christian, I longed for acceptance in a largely Jewish state. I was mostly greeted with suspicious glances and questions. These people had been greatly persecuted by Christians for centuries and were very guarded. I longed for an open door —and then I gave them my name: "Judith." A smile, with a questioning look would cross their faces, followed by the question, "Are you Jewish?" Then I could respond with, "I'm Jewish in my heart." Long before I was born, God had told my parents my name, a name that would reflect my destiny and one of the great loves of my life. God told Jeremiah, "Before I formed you in the womb, I knew you, and before you were born, I consecrated you; I appointed you a prophet to the nations" (*Jr.* 1:5).

The child you are carrying has a destiny and a calling from God. It will take years for that to unfold, but you may be privy to that knowledge, as Mary and Elizabeth were, and hold it in the secret places of your heart. The gift you can give to your unborn child is to prayerfully seek his or her name, the name that is recorded in the heart of God. He says to his own, "I have called you by name, you are mine!"

PRAYING IN PREPARATION
FOR BIRTH

Throughout your pregnancy, you have been praying for your baby and for yourself. The last trimester is a good time to start praying for the time of birth. You have been both a home and a source of life for your little one. You have taken great care to do everything right to ensure the well-being of your baby. Now, the time is coming for your baby and you to experience together the process and miracle of birth. The longing to see and hold your precious baby has grown stronger all during this time. Waiting seems almost unbearable, the months so long. During our second pregnancy, David was two weeks beyond the doctor's projected birth date; he had his own timetable. Everyone kept calling to see how we were, and asking, "Isn't that baby ever going to be born?" Within us, the excitement and longing grew. As we waited, we found great peace reading the Scriptures, especially *Psalm* 27:14:

> Wait for the Lord;
> be strong, and let your heart take courage;
> yes, wait for the Lord!

This prayer became our comfort—helping us realize that God was in complete control, and His unseen hand was making ready the right moment.

> We know that in everything God works for good
> with those who love him, who are called according
> to His purpose *(Rm.* 8:28).

We placed the longing and the waiting in His care and asked Him to appoint the time when everything would come together perfectly for the time of birth. Then we rested, knowing that all was well.

I would like to suggest to those of you preparing for birth that you prayerfully consider taking courses in natural childbirth. They are usually offered through the hospital or local community clinics. Even if you are reluctant to consider natural childbirth, the training proves beneficial during labor, birth and the time following. The Lord intended the birth process to be natural, and He prepared you and your baby for every phase of it. Unfortunately, in our society, expectant mothers are usually viewed as being sick, and are treated accordingly. The growing emphasis on natural childbirth shifts our thinking from sick and problematic deliveries to natural and healthy ones. There are many different methods of natural childbirth; Lamaze, Bradley, Dick-Read, to mention a few. The emphasis of each one is that you can experience childbirth as a normal but strenuous activity similar to an athletic event; like any athletic activity, it requires dedicated preparation. In addition, the goal is to help you eliminate destructive fear, tension and pain. You will be taught exercises, such as breathing control and muscle relaxation, and will be given information about how to help yourself and your baby.

The greatest help, in my opinion, is the support that these methods offer your husband or close friend who will be trained to guide, reassure and assist you during labor and birth. Francis and I took these classes for both of our babies, and he remained with me throughout the labor, delivery and the time following. His reassuring presence, guidance and prayers were extremely helpful, and enabled me to have a natural birth both times. This shared experience of bringing our babies into the world in a natural way (and with prayer) has been without doubt our greatest joy as a couple. There are many different philosophies about childbirth, and several alternatives for you to choose from, so you should be able to find one that is compatible with your desires and needs. Discussing these decisions with your doctor or midwife early in your pregnancy is advisable. For our second birth, we found a wonderful Christian obstetrician and midwife, who formed our team. We selected a birthing suite in the hospital, which afforded us a homey atmosphere and a place where our friends could join us in praying for the birth. (This is even better than a birthing room where you stay only during labor and not for the birth itself.) Within sixteen hours after entering the hospital, we returned home with our new little son, who never left our presence following his birth. Very different from the days when a mother was kept in the hospital ten days to two weeks, rarely seeing her baby, while the father was treated as an outsider. A beautiful bonding experience occurs in this type of natural, homelike environment, where mother and father can be present to share the miracle of birth.

If you have fears relating to childbirth which might prevent you from sharing a joyful, natural experience, pray with your husband about the root cause of these fears so you can be set free.

"CAN A MOTHER FORGET HER SUCKING CHILD?" (IS. 49:15)

We need to discuss nursing here in the third trimester rather than in the chapter on birth, because the mother needs to make a decision about breast-feeding her child long before birth in order to prepare her breasts. When David was born I had recently finished nursing Rachel (who had nursed for more than a year), and I thought I was prepared, but I experienced some pain, particularly in one breast, because, even in that short time, my nipples had again grown tender. Nursing is such a blessing to both mother and child that I hope you will choose breast-feeding—and prepare for it. It is a practice which is once again favored by mothers after falling out of style earlier in our century.

God knew the strong, loving bond that exists between a mother and her nursing baby when He gave us this illustration in Isaiah as the strongest example of human love. He compared this tender human relationship to His own great love for each of us, stating that even if a nursing mother should forget her child, He would never forsake us. A newborn baby needs to feel the warmth and closeness of her mother. Since touch is the way love is communicated to the baby in the first days of her life, what better way of touching and nurturing your little one than by breast-feeding. Nursing offers your baby the reassurance of feeling your arms, hearing your heartbeat and having the deeply satisfying experience of sucking. I found nursing our babies one of my most joyful times, even at night. Very little can compare with the tender, loving feelings I felt for each child as I rocked and nursed them. To know that God had so prepared my body to produce milk for my little one remains a miracle to me. Special hormones are released in your body when you are nursing. One lactation hormone, prolactin, produces in the mother a longing for contact that is best soothed by nursing her baby. Another hormone, oxytocin, is produced to help release the milk. This hormone relaxes the mother and opens the ducts to make her milk ready for the baby. Nursing is satisfying, to the mother as well as to the baby.

Studies conducted on institutionalized babies that lack consistent loving and nurturing show, as Selma Fraiberg writes, that when these babies grow up, they are "unable to form stable human bonds, unable to love. The human capacity for empathy, for feeling oneself into another personality, was absent. Many of them became men and women who seemed to have no pleasure in body intimacy and whose sexual appetites were impoverished or bizarre. Aggression, which is normally modified in the early years through the agency of love, appeared in these loveless men and women in erratic forms."[9] The question therefore that must be asked is, "What transpires between a baby and her parents that enables her to be a loving, trusting adult?" I believe a most important factor is the miracle of intimacy which occurs between the baby and her mother during the months of nursing. The baby feels the mother's loving arms, is satisfied in her craving for nourishment and recognizes her mother's face. These pleasurable feelings all work together to give the baby a sense of being loved and cared for. These strong bonds with the mother allow the baby later in life to trust and love, and therefore to form intimate, loving relationships. The same results can come about through bottle-feeding if the baby is held, as in the ancient traditional way of nursing. Unfortunately, many mothers who bottle-feed find that time does not allow them to hold their babies, and so the baby experiences separation from her mother, either because the mother props the bottle, or several caretakers feed the baby. "In many busy households," Fraiberg said, "the baby is fed by means of a propped-up bottle and is deprived of the vital nutrients of love. Alone with her bottle in the crib, she will not learn to associate feeding with body intimacy and the face of her mother. And in cases where a baby is fed during her bottle feeding by someone other than her mother, she may not associate feeding with pleasure and intimacy in relation to a central person which disturbs the conditions for the love bonds."[10]

To convey love to your baby, and to insure her ability to love and bond with others later in life (whether she is breast-fed or bottle-fed), you must give her the feeling that you love and care for her. You are her primary source, her need-satisfier, during these crucial years of development. God has equipped you, biologically, emotionally and spiritually, so that you can be the source of life for her. You will never have another time in your life when you will be so needed and so accepted. If you need to talk with someone about questions concerning breast-feeding your baby, the most supportive and informative group I found was the La Leche League, which is found in almost every city. I called on them several times in the first few months of nursing and found them very knowledgeable and supportive. They put out an excellent book, *The Womanly Art of Breastfeeding,*[11] which will answer almost any question you have. They also offer weekly meetings in private homes for mothers and their nursing babies. This group support is very important during the early months of nursing.

The progress that is being made in our country to restore natural childbirth and breast-feeding is simply returning a God-given heritage to women. With the support and assistance of a good obstetrician or midwife, you can have a happy, natural delivery and experience the joys and intimacy of breast-feeding. God intended for babies to enter this world without fear and to be greeted by loving parents. This is the way our Lord entered the world, born of a woman, and nursed at her breast. In 1598 in St. Augustine, Florida, a shrine was dedicated to the Mother of Jesus under the title, "Nuestra Senora de la Leche y Buen Parto," which translates freely, "Our Lady of Happy Delivery and Plentiful Milk."[12] This is God's desire for you and your little one—a happy delivery and plentiful milk.

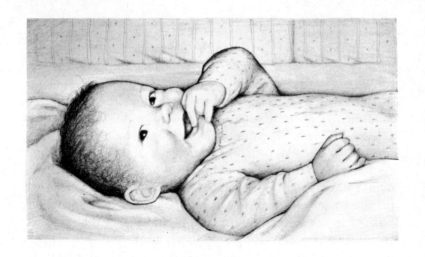

Chapter Eight

GIVING BIRTH

(by Judith)

"THE TIME CAME FOR HER
TO BE DELIVERED . . ."
(LK. 2:6)

After several long hours of labor the doctor held up our first newborn and announced, "It's a girl!" Though I was exhausted after a sleepless night and a day of pushing and panting, a feeling of elation swept over my husband and me. Holding each other and our precious little girl, we tearfully and joyfully thanked God for the miracle of birth. It was a profound spiritual experience for the three of us, one always to be remembered with great joy and love. When the doctor placed Rachel in my arms, I spoke softly to her. All struggling stopped, and she turned her head and looked directly into my eyes. It was not our first meeting, as we had come to know each other during the nine months of waiting. But, we now were, for the first time, discovering each other through our eyes and touch. What I saw in her eyes was a knowing—she knew me, and loved me. Innocent and trusting eyes that didn't need to look away, or reject, or judge; eyes that only wanted to love and be loved. That moment, that loving exchange between mother and daughter birthed in me new depths of loving and caring that I didn't think were possible. Her gentle touch awakened within me a powerful need to protect, nurture and love this tender new life given to us by God.

You will never be the same following the birth of your child. In a moment, your life has changed. You and your husband have become parents, caretakers, entrusted by God with a new life, a new soul. It has been said it only takes a moment to become a mother or a father, but it takes a lifetime to be a parent. Each stage of caring has new challenges, and its own seasons of joy and pain. You have begun a journey in caring, guided by the author of life. Many psychologists believe the birth experience is the most important experience of your child's life, one that will affect her attitude toward self and the world. Patterns for later development will be set during this first experience of meeting the world. Studies reveal that babies with positive, uncomplicated births tend to be more secure, and to get along better in life. Some forms of mental illness, such as depression and suicidal tendencies have been traced to traumatic births. A difficult birth can definitely affect bonding and how the child will later relate to her family. Although controversy still surrounds this subject, parents-to-be should make every effort to ensure an uncomplicated birth experience for their child (and for themselves).

A mother's attitude toward the birth experience is vital to what happens to her and her baby. Women who fear the birth process have more difficulty giving birth, and birth complications occur more frequently with seriously troubled mothers. Dr. Daniel Friedman of Lawrence, N.Y., has done research on parturiphobia, or fear of childbirth, among high school girls. He found that young girls absorb from their elders and peers fearfully distorted accounts of labor and delivery. His study of fifteen-year-olds found that 58 percent already were afraid of childbirth, and 72 percent either knew nothing or had distorted concepts about childbirth. His conclusion? Fear is an all-pervasive factor in childbirth. Women are still concerned about suffering acute pain, undergoing serious body damage or even dying. Only a minority can accept the biological process for what it is. By the time they get to the stage of actually bearing children, they already have a phobia.[1] Of the women I have interviewed, about 95 percent remembered horror stories concerning birth related to them by their mothers or their peers. These exaggerations leave a deep impression on a young woman, and may definitely influence her feelings and attitudes about having her own baby. Unfortunately, her fears, when left in darkness or ignorance, can only grow to possess her. One woman I interviewed had been told repeatedly by her mother that *she*, the daughter, had damaged her mother physically during childbirth and had almost "killed" her. The daughter had been too large for a vaginal delivery and had been stuck in the birth canal for a period of time. Her mother's repeated stories about the pain involved in bringing her to birth and her ensuing guilt at "hurting" her mother and being stuck in the birth canal later resulted in her own irrational guilt and insecurity, a deep-seated fear of childbirth and claustrophobia. When we prayed with this woman for inner healing and asked Jesus to free her from guilt, fear of childbirth and claustrophobia, she experienced a deep healing and was totally freed of those fears.

Dr. Verny states that the mother's maternal attitude is the most critical factor in a healthy birth. His studies indicate that a baby stands a much better chance of growing into an emotionally stable adult if her mother looks forward to her birth.[2] Relaxed, confident mothers tend to have uncomplicated births. On the other hand, he states, "anxious women labor longer than calm ones."[3]

If you remember horror stories about birth, or if you have *excessive* fears about giving birth, it would be good to share them with your husband or a friend, and pray for release and healing. In this way, you can prepare yourself emotionally for a positive birth experience. A simple way of finding out how you really feel about birth is by sharing your thoughts and feelings with your husband; then have him share his feelings with you. It's very important that his attitude also be positive and supportive. Fear or anxiety is easily communicated nonverbally, especially during labor and birth, but you can help rid each other of any excessive fears by talking and praying beforehand. Ideally, this communication and prayer should be done during your pregnancy, not right before birth. Tension and anxiety work against labor and birth; the key to an easy delivery is relaxation. In order to relax, you must be able to trust your partner and the miraculous ways in which God has prepared you and your baby to work together to make birth a beautiful event.

Understanding the biological process of birth will help relieve many of those fears. Some excellent books have been written by doctors, midwifes and experienced mothers on the birthing process. The books I found most helpful were the ones that described, step by step, what would happen from the onset of labor until the time you first nursed your newborn babe. It's important to read a variety of books on the subject since each one differs slightly and offers a different perspective. Birthing is unique, and, similarly, no two books on the subject are alike.

Birth is a journey into the unknown and remains somewhat a mystery, and even the birth of each of your own children will affect you differently. What I learned in my reading and sharing with other mothers and with doctors helped dispel some of the biological mystery of birth, and enabled me to understand what was happening to my body and to our baby. Learning to cooperate with the biological process is extremely beneficial—otherwise your body will offer resistance due to your fears and tensions. When you are centered on what is happening to your body, you can participate in the birth experience—otherwise, you are merely a spectator.

The more you try to control what is happening, or escape from it, the more you will fear losing control. While I was in the hospital, awaiting the birth of our first child, we were placed in a very pleasant, small labor room. We were left alone most of the time, and the doctor only appeared once during labor. In the two labor rooms adjoining ours, two very different labors were occurring. One very young teenager was giving birth, and had arrived at the hospital very near transition. She was alone and fearful. She screamed constantly and called out for help. Our hearts and our prayers went out to her. She knew nothing about the birth process or what was happening to her. She continued to scream throughout the birth, but, happily, gave birth to a lovely, healthy baby girl. What effect her birth experience had on her and her baby I do not know. In contrast, the other labor room was occupied by a young couple giving birth to their first child. They had taken natural childbirth classes, and the husband was coaching his wife. At every contraction he would yell in his loudest, most authoritative voice—"PUSH!" It was so loud and so forceful, that I almost pushed listening to him. Each time he would yell, Francis and I would have to cover our mouths for fear of laughing too loud. This young husband was definitely taking his coaching job very seriously. He was so anxious, though, I'm not sure how much he was able to help his wife relax.

Learning to cooperate with the biological process of labor will increase your chances for a relaxed birth experience for you and your baby. The entire process is designed by God and is largely independent of your will or control. You cannot make it start, and you cannot make it stop; it flows at its own speed and rhythm. You will experience your body functioning on its own to bring forth life. The truly miraculous way God has designed your body to carry your baby has already become clear to you, and now you can experience the numerous ways he has prepared your body to bring your baby forth into the world. For example, in preparation for your baby's birth, you may begin to feel Braxton-Hicks contractions, a tightening or hardening of your uterus designed to tune up your uterus and prepare it for active labor. Your cervix starts to soften so that it can be dilated by the contractions of labor. Many women dilate a few centimeters before active labor begins. Your joints relax in response to the huge amounts of hormones the placenta manufactures to produce more give in the pelvic area, through which your baby must pass. Your breasts begin to produce colostrum, which your baby will live on for the first days of her life before your regular milk starts to flow.

You may also notice puffiness in your fingers, feet or face. This is due to placental hormones causing you to retain fluids so you do not become dehydrated during labor. One young pregnant woman I talked with recently was complaining about her "puffy fat feet." She didn't know this was God's way of ensuring that her body had enough fluid during labor. You will also have 50 percent more blood circulating through your body, a safeguard during birth, when some blood loss is unavoidable.

These are just a few of the marvelous ways God has designed your body to prepare for the birth of your child. Learning about these biological preparations helps you appreciate and cooperate with what is happening within you.

God's design is also evident during the actual labor and birth; a miracle is taking place within you. All you need to do is cooperate with it. The uterus has become the largest muscle in your body by the time your labor begins. The uterine contractions serve several purposes. During early labor, each contraction allows the uterine ligaments to pull up on themselves gradually, drawing the cervix apart, taking it up into the uterine wall itself. At the same time, pressure at the top of the uterus (the fundus) presses the baby farther down into the pelvic basin, speeding the opening of the cervix and hastening the time for actually pushing the baby out. The labor contractions repeat a pattern of working and resting, working and resting, over and over again. They start slowly and gently, then intensify and lengthen as labor progresses.

Labor itself is divided into three stages: 1) the flattening and opening of the cervix, 2) birth, and 3) afterbirth.

The first stage 1) includes early labor (usually considered a warmup time, with slow progress), 2) active labor (when much progress is made and the contractions grow stronger and longer), and 3) transition (the final dilation of the cervix, accompanied by stronger contractions with very short, if any, intervals between). During the second stage, birth, the baby moves through the open cervix aided by the body's contractions, which the mother can help by pushing. An urge to push, continuous, or on and off, usually accompanies each contraction. The third stage (afterbirth) allows for the placenta, water sac and umbilical cord to pass out of the mother's body. As you can see from this brief description of the process of birthing, your body is designed by God to bring forth life in a natural way. The best thing you can do is to learn to cooperate with the process and relax. The various birthing philosophies are designed to help you find a method that is compatible with your needs and beliefs.

What is happening to your baby during labor? And birth? Your baby has enjoyed nine months of blissful floating in your womb. Her environment has been nonthreatening and pleasant. Suddenly, everything changes when labor begins, and her world is altered. Rhythmic contractions are now pushing and squeezing the baby, forcing her to leave her comfortable home. Dr. Verny describes the birth experience as the "first prolonged emotional and physical shock the child undergoes."[4] It is viewed as an interruption, and not necessarily a pleasant one. The baby will now have to cope with tremendous psychological and physical changes. Birth will have a profound and lasting influence on your baby. Though medical advances have decreased the dangers of childbirth, it is still, from your baby's point of view, a perilous journey into the unknown.

How much will your baby remember of her birth experience? Recent studies on birth memories indicate that some people have nearly total recall of the events surrounding their births. These studies (although for most people these memories are subconscious), provide evidence that your baby's mind is recording her birth, and these memories affect her the rest of her life. Children between the ages of two and three are often able to recall their births. After three or four, these memories seem to drop permanently from their consciousness. When our little girl, Rachel, was three years old, I asked her if she remembered her birth. She had several memories which indicated some recall. Her first response was: it felt like swimming. When questioned further, she said it also felt like exercise, and she became very tired. She also remembered a bright light. Now that Rachel is five, I have questioned her again, but she can't remember any details of her birth.

Dr. Verny states that "birth produces a kind of amnesic effect; there is good reason to believe that it does so because of the oxytocin (the female body's principal hormone for inducing uterine contractions and lactation) secreted by the mother during labor and birth. Recent studies show that oxytocin induces amnesia in laboratory animals, so it may be that the presence of this hormone accounts for the fact that so many birth memories slip from our conscious recall."[5] Simply because we can't remember our birth experiences doesn't indicate they can't affect us later in life in positive or negative ways. Dr. David Chamberlain, a clinical psychologist, became interested in birth memories in 1975 when one of his clients traced existing problems to a traumatic birth experience. Since that time, Dr. Chamberlain has studied and documented one hundred cases of birth and womb memories which have led him to conclude that babies are very much aware of what is happening to them during the birth process.[6] Dr. Verny states that neurological memory is present at the beginning of the last trimester, indicating that actual experiences are, by then, being recorded by the brain. He believes, however, that evidence is growing of some sort of a nonneurological memory system.[7] From our experiences in praying with people, we believe that somehow we can remember a few things that go all the way back to conception. *How* that can happen is scientifically problematic, but perhaps some impressions are recorded in the *spirit* of the child—that spirit which is created by God and is eternal. The spirit is nonphysical, and therefore may not have to rely on the development of cells and neurological networks. At any rate (however we may explain it), several people have been able to recall, while Francis and I were praying, something that was missing or wrong in their conception that God needed to heal and set right.

The memories of your baby's birth experience, whether consciously or unconsciously remembered, will have a lasting effect on the person she becomes. For that reason, every effort should be made to minimize any possible difficulties in giving birth. The term "cooperative childbirth" reflects your need to cooperate with the biological process when you bring your baby into the world. The entire birth process involves tremendous physiological and psychological changes for your baby. During labor, uterine contractions force her head deeper into the birth canal, meeting the resistance of the bones of your pelvis and of the slinglike pelvic floor. As she moves downward, her head rotates naturally as it moves farther into the birth canal. Many people, in documented birth memories, recall being stuck in the birth canal, leading to a fear of suffocation. Stanislav Grof reports that thousands of his clients have recalled the trauma of impending suffocation that often accompanies the constriction of the umbilical cord or compression of the infant's body during delivery. Head pain is frequently associated with birth trauma, says gynecologist David Cheek. If patients are simply able to recall and talk about the painful pressure to their heads during birth, that alone is often enough to eliminate the symptoms of chronic headache, including migraine.[8]

We cannot emphasize strongly enough how important it is to pray for the mother and baby during the active stage of labor and birth. Although birth is a natural biological process, problems can occur which need to be brought to the Lord in prayer.

Familiarizing yourself with what is happening to your baby, and with the meaning of certain medical terms, can help, too. During active labor with Rachel, the doctor appeared, examined me, announced Rachel was in "fetal distress" and disappeared. We weren't certain what that actually meant, but we knew it didn't sound good. We prayed together for her, and then Francis went to the waiting room where our dear friends Dan and Mary Wright were waiting and praying during my labor. Francis told them what the doctor had said, and they joined in praying for us. This bond of love and prayer support was so important to us. To have someone in the waiting room who can stay there and then phone your friends when you go into labor is very supportive, both emotionally and spiritually.

We learned later that Rachel was in fetal distress because she was turned around. Fetal distress is caused when the baby is not getting enough oxygen because of forceful or prolonged contractions. It shows itself in the baby's slowed heartrate. When we learned her position wasn't right, we started praying that she would turn, and I assumed certain positions that would enable her to turn more easily. The doctor announced that he would have to use forceps to turn her if she didn't turn by herself. After we prayed, Rachel turned to the proper position for birth without the aid of forceps. As in all things during the birth, we then thanked God that Rachel's birth had not needed forceps.

Praying for each stage of labor and delivery calls the assistance of God into your birth process, and brings you and your baby peace and strength. I felt throughout the birth process the strength and encouragement of my husband and friends, and also the presence of the Lord, assuring me that all was well. I knew He was in control, directing each step of the way. More importantly, I knew He was with our baby, bringing her strength and help.

Naturally, you should continue to pray after your baby is born. Many physiological changes are occurring within the baby that are extremely important for her well-being. She is beginning to breathe on her own for the first time. Up until this time her lungs have been full of fluid, and her first breath is very difficult—it may come with or without a cry. Neither one of our babies cried, but I could tell how difficult it was to take the first breath. With that first breath, your baby loses dependence on the placenta, and turns pink as the oxygen fills her little lungs. This is a wondrous occasion, full of great emotion for the parents. The environmental temperature changes from a warm, 98-degree womb, to a sometimes too cold, delivery room. This is a good reason to ask that your baby be placed directly on your breast as soon as possible. You are probably the most radiant source of heat in the room; furthermore, you and your baby can be together. Your baby will have to begin to cope with all kinds of different functions at birth—breathing, eliminating, eating, plus changes in light, gravity, cold and noise. For these reasons, try to get subdued lighting and reduce the noise.

The way your newborn looks is very different from the way most people imagine she will look. She is covered with white, greasy vernix; she will probably be gray in color until she starts to breathe, and her head may be misshapen for a time due to its being molded as it passes through the birth canal. She may also have a flat nose and ears, and any number of marks and bruises. The reality is that a newborn does not look like a Gerber baby, and you can prepare yourself for that shock by looking at photographs or movies of an actual birth.

I believe newborns are beautiful, but they do look very different from what most people envision. My father was present at my birth because it took place in our home in Jackson, a small town in Kentucky. The hospital was fifty miles away, so it was decided my mother shouldn't make the trip over the bumpy mountain roads. During labor, many supportive women were with my mother, and, following my birth, several neighbors rushed in to celebrate my new life. It was a time of great rejoicing and thanksgiving! When the country doctor handed me to my father, he took one look at me and said, "She sure is ugly!" Somehow those words and the perceived rejection found a place in my mind. This contributed, later in life, to my distorted self-image. Most of the time, I felt good about the way I looked, but, on occasion, there was a small threatening voice inside me that would whisper, "She sure is ugly." I lacked freedom in this area of my mind. Then, when I was in my twenties and living in Israel, my father came to visit me. One morning as we were having breakfast, I again asked him about my birth. He repeated the story and ended by reminding me of what an ugly baby I had been. When he said that, I felt crushed and wounded; I wanted to cry, and I felt ugly! I recognized immediately that this was the lie and the pain I had lived with since birth: my father's response at my birth had affected me for twenty-eight years. When he looked up from his breakfast he saw the pain and tears in my eyes. Since my father is a very loving, sensitive man, he was immediately concerned that he had hurt me. I said, "Did you really think I was ugly when I was born?" I felt like a child at that moment; I hadn't realized the source of those ugly feelings that I had lived with so many years. He said, very tenderly, "I only thought you were ugly for a few minutes." Then we both had a good laugh at his honesty. Afterward he said, "You were the most beautiful baby any father could have prayed for, and you are so beautiful now!" His words were spoken with such love and gentleness, I felt the Lord's presence and His love (and my father's love) washing over the pain which that little baby who was still inside me had felt. Dad gave me a big hug and said, "Forgive me if I hurt you; I love you very much!" With that forgiveness and the Lord's healing love, I was freed that day from a sense of rejection and ugliness.

The most important gift you can give your child at birth is your love—unconditional, unlimited and undefiled. Babies born into a loving, accepting home, tend to view the world also as a warm, welcoming home. They are disposed to *trust*, which will enable them throughout life to enter into loving relationships with God, others and themselves. Their foundation is solid, and the storms of life will not be able to damage it. Your loving touch will calm and assure your little one that you are there to protect, nurture and love her. Touching is your baby's way of "feeling your love." During the time in your womb, your baby was constantly stimulated by the amniotic fluid and by the womb itself. Dr. Ashley Montagu states in his book *Touching* "that the uterine contractions of labor constitute the beginning caressing of the baby in the right way—a caressing which should be continued in very special ways in the period immediately following birth and after."[9]

Babies, following birth, *need* to be placed in the mother's arms, or on her body, not only for warmth, but for her loving touch, to comfort and console. Birth is the time when mother, child and father *need* to be together. Childbirth experts believe that the way a woman feels emotionally and physically during pregnancy and delivery, coupled with the amount of *contact* she has with her baby directly afterward, strongly affects her "motherliness"—her feelings about being a mother. Unfortunately, the American way of childbirth is insensitive to these feelings. "Most civilized countries wouldn't think of routinely separating mothers and babies directly after birth (as we do) and keeping them apart merely to suit hospital practices."[10]

Loneliness begins early in babies who are separated from their parents. That premature separation could be a main source of the loneliness that permeates our society. In my private counseling practice, I discovered that many of my clients suffered from deep feelings of loneliness. How much of it started at birth when they were routinely separated from their mothers and placed in a cold, brightly lit nursery with dozens of other screaming, lonely babies? When you think about it, it seems ridiculous to take a baby away from the mother who has been her home and source of life for nine months. The time immediately after birth is a time when the baby needs to be together with the mother and father. You will feel a need to hold and cuddle your baby—this feeling is natural and God-given. Baby and mother comfort each other. As a mother, you will feel a sense of loss if your baby is taken from you, even for several hours, much less days. After all you've been through, you need to hold and rest *with* your baby—not be alone with empty arms and an empty womb. Once you understand the importance of this time together, you may have to shop around to find a hospital or obstetrician that will allow it. We had to look

for an obstetrician, a midwife team and a hospital that would
not separate us after birth. David never left the room where he
was born, because we found the right doctor and midwife team,
plus a birthing suite in the hospital. (We were fortunate in finding an obstetrician and midwife who wanted to work together.)
Your baby experiences her first real separation when she comes
out of your body, and has her umbilical cord cut. That's enough
separation to bear; aside from that, your baby needs to be with
you and her father.

    Babies who are routinely separated at birth or babies who
are separated due to medical complications, or adoption, need
to be prayed for in special ways; otherwise, feelings of rejection
and fear can envelop the little one. Dr. Frank Lake believes that
the two most common birth catastrophes are asphyxiation feelings and separation anxiety.[11] It is comforting to remember that
Jesus suffered in the same way; he felt asphyxiated when he
struggled for breath during the crucifixion; at the same time, he
suffered the anxiety of being abandoned by his friends and his
Father. "My God, why hast thou forsaken me?" *(Mt.* 27:46) A
little baby feeling alone and abandoned needs the help and
presence of Jesus with his understanding heart. One lady who
had attended a Christian conference where we were speakers
wrote us a beautiful letter describing how Jesus healed her of a
traumatic birth memory dealing with separation. (Incidentally,
the topic of our conference had nothing to do with the unborn
child; we were teaching on the healing of rejection.)

    "On the night when there was a teaching on rejection,
followed by a prayer for inner healing, I was marvelously
healed! When we were asked to pray about what the Lord
would like to heal in us, the image that came to me was me in
my mother's womb. After being prayed for, while resting in the
Spirit, I saw the most beautiful healing take place. The scene
was the hospital delivery room, where Jesus was there with my

mother and the doctor. Jesus was gently urging me to 'be born.'
I distinctly heard him say, 'Nan, it is OK—I will be with you, you
don't need to be afraid of being born.' (I was afraid of being born
since I was three months premature and only weighed three
pounds.) Jesus kept reassuring me I would be all right. Then I
had a sense of being born; Jesus was there holding me, comforting and loving me. Later while I was in the incubator for six
weeks, I saw Jesus caressing and loving me. During the healing
the melody 'Clair de Lune,' by Claude Debussy, was being
played in the background.

"When I returned home from the conference, I shared my
healing experience with my mother. When I told her about
hearing the music, she said it was no wonder that song was such
a comfort to me, because when she was pregnant with me, the
girl in the adjoining apartment played 'Clair de Lune' on the
piano daily. (Maybe that's why that particular piece continues
to be a favorite of mine.) The most beautiful part is that, until I
received this healing prayer, I had always felt unwanted and
unloved. I remember quite clearly, as a toddler, feeling unloved. My mother was almost in tears as I told her this. She said
she and dad were not allowed to hold me until I was six weeks
old! They had to look at me through a window. Mom also said
she never saw the nurses caressing the premature babies in the
incubators. Thanks be to God: for the first time in twenty-four
years I feel loved and cared for. I also have found that my fear of
crowds has left me."

This letter beautifully illustrates how the love of Jesus heals
us when we pray. If your baby *has* to be separated from you for
medical reasons, you can pray and ask Jesus to be there to bring
the comfort and love your little one needs. Your prayers can
bridge the space between you and your baby if she is separated
from you. Some hospitals, becoming aware of the need for the
baby to be held, have brought women into the "preemie" unit

whose function is rocking, serenading and loving the infants. These women have name tags that say "Cuddler." How wonderful it would be if they would learn to add prayer to this cuddling.

During the nineteenth century, more than half the infants in the first year of life regularly died from a disease called marasmus, a Greek word meaning "wasting away."[12] I have seen evidence of this disease in my work as a therapist. The baby is not touched, handled or caressed and literally begins to waste away. Oftentimes both mother and child need the healing love of God to return life and hope to their bodies and spirits.

"It was Dr. Fritz Talbot of Boston who brought the idea of 'Tender, Loving Care' back with him from Germany," Ashley Montagu writes, "While in Germany, Dr. Talbot visited at the Children's Clinic in Dusseldorf, where he was taken through the wards by Dr. Arthur Schlossmann, the director. The wards were very neat and tidy, but what piqued Dr. Talbot's curiosity was the sight of a fat old woman who was carrying a very measly baby on her hip. 'Who's that?' inquired Dr. Talbot. 'Oh, that,' replied Schlossmann, 'is Old Anna. When we have done everything we can medically for a baby, and it is still not doing well, we turn it over to Old Anna, and she is always successful.' "[13]

I'm sure many of you can remember the comfort and healing touch of your mother or father, or the reassurance and sense of well-being you feel when someone you love (and who loves you) touches you. Many times when our children are sick, after we pray, they want mommy to hold and rock them. In my opinion, prayer and loving are still the best medicines—especially, as with Old Anna, when all else has failed. This may be why Jesus said, "They will lay their hands on the sick; and they will recover!" *(Mk.* 16:18) Touching conveys life, caring and the healing power of God. How much more that gentle touch means to an infant, who is unable to communicate with words. Your loving touch will soothe all fear and confusion, bringing peace and comfort to your little one. Try to do all you can to be with her; make those necessary arrangements ahead of time. If separation is unavoidable, pray, asking Jesus to be there with your little one, holding her in his loving arms, until such time as you can.

As I stated in the last chapter, breast-feeding is very important to you and your baby. Your newborn needs to be held close, to feel your warmth and hear your heartbeat. She needs to touch and be touched, and to see your loving face. She will feel cradled by your arms, and warmed by your body. What better assurance of being loved can your baby feel than by touching your body as she nurses. Nursing is such an intimate moment for you and your baby to get to know each other through your eyes, your touch and your nurturing. Several times, as our babies grew older, I had wonderful, loving exchanges while they nursed. One evening, after a nice warm bath, David made his special little sound which meant it was nursing time. As I cradled him in my arms, smelling his sweetness, and gazing on his joyful, contented face, I felt such great love and joy! My heart was full of love for him and thanksgiving to God. Suddenly, David opened his eyes, stopped nursing and, with milk running down his chin, reached out one little, soft hand to caress my face. He smiled and giggled, then returned to his bedtime snack, still cradling my cheek in his baby hand. This incident, and countless others, when I nursed my sleepy, fussy, or sick baby, are among the most memorable, joyful moments of my life.

And it all begins at birth. Those first awkward moments when first-time mother tries to get her child to suckle—mother and baby helping each other to do what God, long ago, so beautifully ordained.

Chapter Nine

TO THE FATHER:
A WORD OF
ENCOURAGEMENT

(by Francis)

Your love has created a new life, and you are sharing in God's own creation of a little person who in some ways will reflect you. It's an adventure, a time to experience the combined joy and pain which are at the heart of every new birth. This much you know.

But it's hard for a father to realize how important he is to that little unborn child developing unseen within his wife's body. You may be mystified by the changes taking place in her body and you can easily assume that childbearing is a world you can watch but not enter into. Your wife directly feels the little life growing within her, while all you can do is share from outside by listening to what she tells you. She may experience bewildering mood changes that she cannot explain to you. At such times you may feel like walking away until things settle down. Few men in our culture learn, as they grow up, how to share their feelings—their pain, their sadness and grief, or even their joys. For nearly thirty years, I never wept because I had learned it was unmanly. Even when my father died, about all I could express at the time was a single, muffled sob; it was as if the wellsprings of my emotions had dried up. Only later did I begin to get in touch with my feelings again—and become capable of expressing grief.

This inability of many men to express feelings makes for a real problem because the wife usually wants to share her feelings, and yet she may find it hard to talk with her husband. This lack of communication can kill love and eventually the marriage itself. When a wife commits adultery the primary reason is usually not sexual attraction, but because she has found a sympathetic man with whom she can share her feelings. Men often seem able to share intimately when they are dating, in the glow of falling in love, but then, later, unless they are careful, they revert to their traditional strong, silent role—finding it hard to share feelings, except for an occasional outburst of anger. Men often seem embarrassed to share what they feel (women seem to share feelings much more easily), and they may be tempted to withdraw into their own world of work, friends or TV.

Yet, now that your wife is pregnant, she needs to draw close to you. It's a wonderful time to learn to share at a deeper level than ever before.

Until I began studying about the unborn child, I did not realize that, *next to the mother's love for her child, the father's love for his wife and the child-to-be is the most important factor*

influencing the child's future happiness. As we have said earlier
in this book, the mother's attitude, her love, joy and peace (all
gifts of the Spirit) profoundly influence the baby's well-being.
But it is your love for your wife, and her being able to experience that love, that envelops her in a peace and joy that give
her the security she needs—which, in turn, is passed on to her
child.[1]

Happily, God has given pregnant women an ability to stand
up well under "situational stress"—the stress that comes from
things going wrong. But the stress that comes from *people*, from
wounded relationships, that kind of stress can reach into the
wife's heart and devastate her. This means that her relation
with her husband has the greatest potential of all to be a blessing, or a curse to her—to strengthen or to weaken her.

Since, as we have seen earlier, the mother's happiness is the
key to her child's happiness, your love for your wife is not only
vital for her but also to your unborn child. Your wife needs your
love and support more than ever at this time. She needs you to
hold her, to share your feelings and hopes and, above all, to pray
with her to bear a happy, healthy child.

It may be hard for you to believe that your unborn child
needs you too. Deep in your heart you know that your love and
concern are vital for your wife's happiness and health; even if
that were the only way you touch your child, that would be
enough. She needs you to hold and cherish her, especially at
times when you are not able to make love. She needs time with
you—quality time—when you can both share your hearts with
each other. When she looks at the growing size of her body in
the mirror she may feel that she is becoming less attractive than
before; she needs to know how much you love her. Now, more
than ever, she needs to be sure that you are faithful to her. In
addition, she may be experiencing morning sickness and is be-
wildered by her unpredictable mood swings.

Share your own hopes and fears about the pregnancy.

Dream together. Listen to each other; just listening—really listening—is one of the most beautiful gifts you can give to each other. Encourage her to share her deepest concerns about the pregnancy. There may be times when fears and worries seem overwhelming: "How will we be able to manage financially?" "My mother told me that my own birth was so painful that, even though she now loves me, she would never go through it all again." "Will I have another miscarriage, as I did last time?"

To all this Jesus has said:

> If a very small thing is beyond your powers, why worry about the rest? Think how the flowers grow; they never have to spin or weave; yet, I assure you, not even Solomon in all his royal robes was clothed like one of them. Now if that is how God clothes a flower which is growing wild today and is thrown into the furnace tomorrow, how much more will he look after you, who have so little faith! But you must not set your hearts on things to eat and things to drink; nor must you worry. It is the gentiles of this world who set their hearts on all these things. Your Father well knows you need them. No, set your hearts on his kingdom, and these other things will be given you as well *(Lk.* 12:25–31, NJB).

At times like this, when your wife's faith falters, your faith can help sustain her. But there may be times, too, when you are the one who needs to be strengthened: perhaps you are worried about whether you will be a good father, or about how you will manage financially; then her strength and prayers may help sustain you. St. Paul encourages us to bear one another's burdens and you can only do that if you tell your wife what's bothering you.

Dr. Jerrold Shapiro did a survey of 227 expectant and recent fathers and found that their fears, like their wives', were very strong—only they were frustrated because they were supposed to be strong and not upset their pregnant wives by talking about their own fears. Among these fears they wondered about whether they would be queasy and become faint or nauseated during the birth. Some of them felt uncomfortable accompanying their wives to the doctor's office; they felt out of place in the examining rooms and were treated coldly by the obstetrical staff, who gave them the impression that they were in the way. Some became worried about the possibility of dying and leaving a widow and orphan(s) behind, to the extent that they became ultracautious in driving their cars. Still others felt that their wives were so wrapped up in the pregnancy that they were losing out in their marriage. A few even engaged in "late pregnancy affairs," usually because they had an intense need to talk about their feelings.[2] These affairs, of course, had a devastating effect upon their marriages; yet, the cause was a perceived rejection by the wife. If husbands would only learn to share these fears with their wives, and pray about them, those same fears would grow less and they would become an occasion of drawing closer to their wives. "One fact that emerged clearly in my study," Shapiro said, "was that when men did share their concerns with their partners, the relationships deepened and closeness increased."[3] I was in my fifties when Judith was pregnant with Rachel and David, so, naturally, I was worried about how I would hold up as a father, whether I could take the toll of being constantly wakened in the middle of the night. (And, it did turn out that, for a period of two years after David was born, we only averaged about three hours' sleep a night.) Much of the time we were traveling and speaking, too, and both Judith and I were physically and emotionally drained. Certainly, it was only God's grace and our prayer for each other that saw us through. So, our concerns were grounded in reality, but we needed Jesus to lay our excessive fears to rest in the trust that he would take care of us, no matter what.

Pregnancy is also a wonderful time for you to pray for inner healing of any event in your wife's past that might, in some way, harm the pregnancy. For instance, if she has heard from her mother (or anyone else) that the pains of birth are almost unbearable, Jesus can set her free, as you pray, from this fear, which can weigh her down during the pregnancy. Her anxieties can complicate the birth by tightening her up and increasing the very pain that she so much fears. It would help for both of you to read any of the fine books on the natural methods of childbirth and learn the exercises that will help ease the unnecessary tensing up of her body. Judith and I read several books, attended Lamaze classes at the hospital and practiced breathing exercises together. All this helped us, not just to ease anxiety but also to look forward with joy to the moment of birth. For me it helped, too, by giving me something I could *do* to help Judith and make the birth *our* birth.

Judith did suffer some pain at birth—especially with Rachel, our firstborn—but it was made more bearable because of all our preparation, and because I was with her to encourage her and, above all, to pray with her for Jesus to sustain her during the most stressful moments during transition.

If there are any past events that might warp your attitude and your wife's toward birth, be sure to pray for inner healing together.[4] One of the special areas where we have found many men (and women, as well) need healing is in their relationship with their fathers. If your father has been harsh, demanding or abusive—or even if he was simply absent or unable to show his love for his children—that harsh or distant relationship later rubs off on the child's image of God the Father. On the human level, the reason many men have difficulty relating to God in a personal way is simply that they had a hard time believing that their earthly fathers truly loved them. Judith and I have seen remarkable breakthroughs when we prayed for healing of men's poor relationships with their fathers; their spiritual lives and relationship with God improved in spectacular ways following their inner healing. So, if you find it hard to pray alone or with your wife, finding a trustworthy person who can pray for your inner healing will help you relate to God, to your wife and to your children.[5] Nothing can bring you closer to each other and to the Lord.

Here are some of the areas where your wife may need healing: any excessive fear about the birth itself; excessive fears about miscarrying; wide mood swings and depression. Some depression is, of course, purely physical, the result of the hormones rapidly changing at this special time, but, even here you can pray that these hormonal changes take place gradually and harmoniously. You, too, may need healing in such areas as having too strong a desire for a child of one sex, to the extent of being grossly disappointed if the baby should, for example, turn out to be a girl; also, some part of you may not really want a child at this time (e.g., for financial reasons). You need to deal with this, because somehow your child will "know" if your love is not wholehearted.

Thirty years ago husbands were kept out of the birthing room and only received the news of the birth from a nurse poking her head out a door to tell them—but those days are happily disappearing. Such enforced separation of father from mother at this crucial, beautiful time encouraged the belief that bearing the child was all the woman's work—that she didn't really need her husband during this great event. We are now coming out of that darkness, out of that practical denial of the meaning of marriage at the moment of birth. But in addition to encouraging fathers to help at the moment of birth, we need to recapture a sense of the couple's oneness all during the months leading up to birth. If your work schedule allows it, plan to accompany your wife on some of her visits to the obstetrician to see how she and your unborn child are progressing. Fortunately, I was able to go with Judith to see her doctor most of the time; those visits were to me the closest, most unforgettable moments in her pregnancies. Even though some of those trips are now six years past, I remember them as if they were yesterday. When we first heard Rachel's heartbeat, it was, to me, meeting her for the first time, and both Judith and I wept at the joy of that faint beat. Later, when we saw Rachel's tiny body on a sonogram, we experienced an overwhelming joy and wonder at God's creation. To me it was very special that I was able to share that moment with Judith—to see our little baby for the first time together, rather than just having her tell me about it at supper that night.

Husbands have also learned in recent years that, during the last three months of the pregnancy, they can talk to the child. The sound waves are carried through the mother's body to the child's developing ear. And while that child will not hear you as clearly as he hears his mother, still he will learn to *recognize your voice.* When the child is born and you speak to him then, he will not be hearing an unfamiliar voice but one which he has come to know and trust. Yours will be a familiar, reassuring voice. (If you and your wife enjoy singing together, so much the better; there are some remarkable stories that indicate that children later recognize music they first heard in the womb.)

If you can possibly attend birthing classes with your wife, be sure to do so. You will be a great support to your wife just in being there to encourage her and to help with the breathing exercises. Judith says that if I had not been with her to help Rachel's birth (it took fourteen hours—about average for a first child), she probably would have had to take an anesthetic toward the end of those hours of labor (she didn't want to take an anesthetic because it affects the baby, and has a depressing effect upon his first hours in this world). If you can find a hospital with a birthing room or, better yet, a birthing suite, so much the better. For David's birth, we found a hospital—an hour from us —with a birthing suite. It was well worth risking the long ride; David was never taken from us, never taken to the nursery, but was allowed to stay in the same room with Judith the entire time of her hospital stay (which was only one day). And I was able to stay with Judith and David in the same room, resting overnight on a couch. That constant presence of the parents makes a great difference in the baby's first impressions of life— and leads to greater trust, security and self-confidence. Later in life that human experience of trust will make it easier for the child to trust God and to develop the divine virtues of faith, hope and love.

While waiting to be born, your little baby is not only physically protected by your wife's body but is spiritually protected by her love and prayer. Both of them, in turn, mother and child, are physically surrounded, as it were, by your strong arms and are spiritually protected by your supportive love and prayer.[6]

God desires your unborn child to draw you closer to your wife with a love stronger than ever before. Each pregnancy, each birth, will leave you with a beautiful, unforgettable memory to cherish for the rest of your days. As you share your wife's pains and anxieties, you will also come to share in her overwhelming joy when your child is born.

> A woman in childbirth suffers, because her time has come; but when she has given birth to the child she forgets the suffering in her joy that a human being has been born into the world (*Jn.* 16:21, NJB).

Chapter Ten

A TESTIMONY

The following is a beautiful testimony describing the kind of healing that we often see the Lord perform. An important part of this story is the healing of the trauma of rejection within the mother's womb. The writer of this letter had suffered from a life-long depression and had always avoided social gatherings because of her basic fear of people. (From our point of view it is significant that, in addition to healing, she also received a deliverance from evil spirits. Our sessions of healing prayer went on for several days and averaged about two hours each.)

"Years of compressed depression are fading away, and the wall between myself and humanity is progressively dissolving. I no longer hit bottom as I did in years past. The healings I received were very deep; God continues to unfold the beautiful wholeness he intended for me from conception.

"The following is a close account of what happened in Florida in 1980 when you both prayed with me."

"6/9/80

"After arriving at my motel in Clearwater I opened Scripture to Isaiah 1:18:

" 'Come now, let us talk this over, though your sins are like scarlet they shall be as white as snow, and though they are red as crimson, they shall be like wool.'

"I also opened to Isaiah 2:22–24:

" 'For God formed man to be imperishable; the image of his own nature he made him. But by the envy of the Devil, death entered the world and they who are in his possession experience it.'

"The Lord spoke to me through these passages, revealing to me that he would heal any of sin's damage within me. I never realized before how vicious Satan is and how he plots to destroy all our potential."

"6/10/80

"I was terrified waiting for Judith to see me. I took three aspirins to calm me down. Once inside the office I told her what was going on inside me. I heard a voice saying to me, 'You're a fool for coming, because nothing is going to happen!' Judith assured me that something was going to happen.

"After we talked, Judith prayed with me.

"To understand what the Spirit revealed, I would like to tell you that God sent me a prophetic dream in 1972, in which I saw a tiny embryo all encased in cement. This infant was thrust out into a violent dirt storm. In the dream the storm lasted two and a half weeks, after which the embryo rested. . . . The dirt settled around the embryo, and a mound of dirt formed and then was overgrown with beautiful green grass. As I watched this dream, a bolt of lightning hit the tiny prisoner and broke the casing loose.

"When Judith prayed for me, this dream came to mind, and I saw the infant lying *outside* the casing. A light came into the scene and shone on the infant. The baby turned pink and then red. I watched the baby receiving new life. A voice came to me and said, 'I sent you as my gift to your parents.'

"At this point I realized how rejected I had felt, and that I wished that I had never been born. Since Judith's prayer I have been slowly "coming to life" and realizing how good it is to live, to have been created . . . to be human, to be flesh and to have the incarnate Word become flesh of my flesh."

"6/11/80

"As Francis and Judith prayed with me in their home, Jesus came to me in the Spirit and led me through the home I was raised in. We went to the basement first, where Jesus stood beside me as we watched my mom doing the washing. Then he took me to the living room and showed me a deep, dark cage with bars of steel, both horizontal and vertical (the cage came out of one of the walls). Jesus then said, 'He can't hurt you anymore.'

"The Lord also took me to the barnyard of our small farm and just stood beside me . . . Then we went down to our raspberry field. As we stood in each of these places I remembered how deeply I had been hurt there. As we went back to these places he healed me of what had happened to me in each place. (In the barnyard, for example, my mother had told my older brother to throw a bushel of rotten tomatoes at me as a punishment. I was thirteen years old and it was such a blow to my meager self-esteem!)

"Still in the Spirit, Jesus and I reentered my home. This time we went up to my room. I was crying because of a terrifying nightmare (they were part of my life until I was about twenty years old). My dad and mom then began to fight because I was crying. Against my mom's wishes Dad came to me, carried me downstairs and rocked me to sleep. As Jesus showed me this scene, my father changed to Abba, God the Father, rocking me in the chair. Even as I type this, it brings me great emotion.

"Francis and Judith prayed with me a second time. This time cries of terror came from me; I remember crying out, 'Please don't beat me, Mama!' I was reliving a terrible beating my mom gave me, after which I gave up on life; I no longer had any desire to go on living. Francis commanded the spirit of Death to leave, and then he rebuked the spirit of Fear.[1] After that Judith asked God to fill all those places in my spirit that had been emptied, with the Holy Spirit."

"6/12/80

"I was staying alone at a Clearwater motel, and I decided to take a walk around town. As I did so Jesus came to me in spirit. Vividly he called to my mind memories of a Monday morning when my poor mother had mounds of dirty clothing to wash. As the oldest girl, I was to assist her; I used to hate this chore and working with her. When Jesus brought this to my mind, Mom was no longer there, but it was Jesus himself helping me do the laundry. He laughed and kept talking to me all the time we worked; I was delighted! Jesus continued doing this all day long, no matter where I went or what I did."

"6/12/80

"Judith could not be present, but Francis prayed for me to be released from the spirit of Rejection. Then I rested in the Spirit.[2] I sensed God the Father, my Abba, putting his arm around me and showing me when I was a small child. He could not get me to love that little child. Finally, I did manage to ask the child if she would forgive me for not loving her all these years. Then Francis prayed a second time. This time I saw the Lord take me and the child to an ice cream parlor. The parlor had three seats in it: one for Jesus, one for me and one for the child (who, of course, was also me, only at a younger age). Jesus put his arms around the two of us, while we ate a delicious chocolate sundae. I looked at the little girl, who was simply delighting in her ice cream; her face and little hands were covered with chocolate ice cream. She looked so funny that I started to laugh. And I began to feel a genuine love for her. Jesus was watching the two of us all this time. At last, he looked at me and said, 'From now on you two are going to get along just fine together!'

"Since this time, my attitude towards myself has changed as much as night and day. The Lord has taught me to minister to myself in a very loving way; as I do so, I am beginning to have a genuine love for other people. This healing has brought me an awe and wonder of being human. God has placed a very special person in my life to reinforce this truth. And what a joy it is to love another person from the heart.

"So much happened that week deep inside me. I only know that I continue to grow in peace about myself, as well as grow in love of others, with a new freedom that I never knew before. I find my memory clearing and a great emotional overload is gradually going away. I am placing a beautiful trust in God also; this trust has led to a new type of free-flowing prayer life within myself.

"Through your compassion, God has rolled the stones away from the tomb that had for so many years held me captive!"

Later in June she wrote us a beautiful follow-up letter, including the following section:

"It seems to me that when darkness reigns within, you do not realize what it's like to be free. Well, I feel great! All my life a mocking ring sounded whenever I tried to love the Lord or carry out my tasks in life. The last time I heard it was just before the spirit of Rejection was cast out. The result: I feel good about myself and my decisions. The other day an angry woman came at me, and, for the first time, her anger never touched me! Wow! It's like being in a dream, hoping that the peace I experience is for real—and forever.

"Socializing has always been an agony for me. But now I feel good about parties and being with people. (I used to make up any excuse, in any situation, to get away from people.)

"One of the greatest changes in me is a new vitality. I do not feel tired all the time, now that Death has been cast out. My whole life has been a war against fatigue. But now, OH, DO I FEEL GOOD!"

Appendix One

THE DEATH OF THE UNBORN: MISCARRIAGE AND ABORTION

(by Francis)

We want to concentrate on the blessings you bring to your unborn child by praying, and, yet, we must face the unpleasant reality of death, our ancient enemy, which may strike down the most innocent victim of all, the unborn child. Some 10 to 20 percent of all pregnancies end in miscarriage, and another 2 percent end in a stillbirth; so, nearly one out of every five mothers will grieve over the loss of her unborn child. If we are realistic, we must at least talk about the possibility of miscarriage, and what we can do to ease the parents' pain if it should happen.

When we add to the tragedy of miscarriage, the million and a half abortions performed every year in the United States (there are now four abortions for every ten live births), we also need to learn how to bring the Lord's healing and love to the woman who has procured an abortion and who later regrets what she had done. Even when she has asked for God's forgiveness and "knows" that she has been forgiven, she may still have a hard time forgiving herself for killing that little life within her. Somehow she may not be able to *feel* in her heart that she is forgiven, even when her faith tells her that God has forgiven her. For such human tragedies, prayer helps provide an answer.

PREVENTION OF MISCARRIAGE

Simply by praying with your partner, you are already helping to cut down on the possibility of a miscarriage. Each time you pray together, your unborn child will absorb some of your love for each other. As the mother is enfolded in her husband's arms and supported by his love, the baby will also be strengthened by that warm embrace. Your baby will mysteriously sense your love. In fact, the love of parents is the single most important spiritual, emotional factor that children pick up in the womb, and it will overcome the negative effects of much stress and anxiety.[1]

Furthermore, while you are praying together (or alone), Jesus will lift much of the fear and apprehension you may be feeling at the prospect of giving birth; this, in itself, will reduce the risk of losing your baby:

> Nearly every emotion a woman has seems to contain a sympathetic dimension. Even feelings with a clear biological basis, such as fear and anxiety, affect a child in ways that go way beyond anything we know about physiology. This is doubly true of emotions that lack any apparent biological anchor, like love or acceptance. Nothing we know about the human body can explain why these feelings affect the unborn child. Yet study after study shows that happy, content women are far more likely to have bright, outgoing infants.[2]

On the other hand, the chances of miscarriage are greatly increased when the mother is excessively *fearful*. If she fears that her husband (or lover) will abandon her, the chances of miscarrying her baby increase—even if she is healthy and there seems to be no medical reason for miscarrying.[3] It's as if the little unborn baby senses the mother's fear of life and decides to opt out of this life rather than face the pain of rejection. Prenatal research indicates that the fear in a fetus may be as great as that in an adult. It seems that every emotion of the mother affects her child. Prolonged stress in the mother—especially the stress of a painful tension with her husband—will stress the fetus too. Somehow, that little baby senses his mother's distress and responds. If exposed to severe, prolonged stress, the fetus may become ten times as active as normal. Several amazing incidents are on record of how the mother was warned in a dream by her baby, who was about to miscarry; and, shortly afterward, the miscarriage took place.[4]

What better thing, then, can parents do, to ensure a safe birth, than to pray together for their unborn child? (If the husband can't join in the prayer, then the mother should, of course, pray alone for their child.) This prayer will draw them closer together both spiritually and emotionally. If there are severe tensions in the marriage itself, the couple needs to work out these problems as well as to pray for each other; they need to forgive one another and pray for inner healing.[5] It's amazing, but you will have a hard time praying with each other if you hold anything against each other. You will have to leave your gift at the altar and go back and be reconciled with each other.[6] If you can humble yourself and ask forgiveness for anything you have done to hurt your partner, you will help your marriage tremendously. If you harbor resentment, you are not only hurting your partner, but also yourself and your child. Do whatever you can to be reconciled, and try to live harmoniously for your unborn baby's sake as well as your own.

Here, it is important to note that *90 percent of married*

couples run into serious marital difficulty within months after the death of a child—primarily because of their inability to share their grief.[7] The best protection against this kind of tragic breakup comes from your sharing deeply in prayer. If you share your hopes and feelings with each other and with the Lord— then, chances are, if you should lose your child, you will be able to weather the storm more easily than a couple that has not been sharing or praying together.

Best of all, praying together will act as a wonderful preventive medicine, protecting both you and your child and preparing you for a safe and happy birth.

THE MOTHER'S GRIEF

If you have ever had a miscarriage, you know how painful such a loss can be. You really can't share your loss, because no one can feel the separation as keenly as you do. For months you have sensed the baby living within you, flesh of your flesh, an intimate part of your life. And yet, for your husband, for your other children and for your friends, your baby is still something of a stranger—someone they have not seen or felt. To them, your baby is still not altogether real, hidden as he is.

A mother's affection for her child develops very early in the pregnancy; studies show that her grief when she miscarries is almost as intense as her pain when a baby dies after it has been born. Yet doctors and friends may treat her loss as lightly as a cold—"You can always have another one, you know"—as if the baby were some anonymous blob of tissue.

Her loss is not a light one. We need to know that, after a miscarriage, the mother usually goes through a period of intense mourning for four to six months, followed by further grieving for the next half year. (If this grief is not moderated or healed, she will be too distracted and sorrowful to bond joyfully with her next child if she becomes pregnant within a year after miscarrying.) She will ordinarily experience shock, disorganization, guilt, anger and loneliness, all of which—if she can't talk and share her pain with someone—can readily lead her into a prolonged depression.

Her grief is especially strong because the baby was so intimately part of her for so long. Yet, no one else can share her sorrow—unless they have been through the same loss, or are extraordinarily sensitive. Chances are, she has no one to talk to about her loss; even her husband, who should be her closest support in her crisis, may not sense the depth of her sorrow, nor be able to share in it. How can he? Just having him listen to her would be a help, but she may feel so depressed that she doesn't feel like talking with him about it. On his part, he may avoid talking about the miscarriage simply because he doesn't know what to say. Worse yet, he may think he is helping by telling her, "Forget it. Let's move on and have another one." Grief intensifies when there is no way of getting it out into the open to talk about it. But who can she talk to? If one of her living children died, all kinds of friends would come forward to offer their sympathy and support. But with a miscarriage, the baby's death is almost like a secret. There is usually no funeral service. No expression of grief. So the mother grieves alone.

Since she has no concrete image of the child to say goodbye to, she feels incomplete and a great emptiness. She is saying goodbye to a child she never held in her arms. For this reason, it may be helpful for the parents (if possible) to see and touch the miscarried child, to name and baptize him and perhaps to hold a simple funeral.

She may also feel guilt and anger over what she (or others) failed to do to preserve the child's life. Every normal mother has some negative feelings about bearing a child because of the unpleasantness of morning sickness, quitting a job and all of the other discomforts that may go with childbearing. Therefore, she may feel guilty that she wasn't the perfectly loving mother, and may feel that her insufficiencies actually led to her losing the child. On the contrary, such feelings of guilt show how much she really wanted to have the child.

How wonderful it is, then, when expectant parents pray together, not only to help prevent miscarriage, but also so that the father can share with the mother and bond with the little child within. If the fetus should, unfortunately, miscarry, the husband can share in his wife's pain and accompany her in the grieving process. She can then share her pain with him more easily and bring her sorrow out of the shadows into the light. Just as every morning and evening they have prayed together for their child, now they can pray for each other and ask Jesus to send his healing and encouragement after their baby's death.

Sharing her grief with her husband will shorten her period of mourning and help avoid the marital problems that usually follow such a loss. If she can't share her feelings with her husband, at least she can open up to a close friend, especially if the friend is another mother who has been through a similar loss.

The ideal arrangement is when her husband (or friend) can not only talk and share her feelings of emptiness and loss, but can also pray for Jesus to heal the pain caused by the baby's death.

HOW TO PRAY FOR
YOUR MISCARRIED CHILD

Here are a few suggestions as to how a husband can pray *with* his wife for the baby they lost. (Since so few husbands seem to pray with their wives, she may have to pray alone, or with a trusted friend.)

1) The first step in prayer is to find a quiet place to pray. Telephone off the hook. Children out of the room. A place where you can really concentrate.

2) Then ask Jesus to come and be present to you with all his love and power. It is amazing how often, as we led this prayer, the mother actually senses the presence of Jesus; sometimes she "sees" him.[8] We don't know how this happens. We just know that it is so.

3) Then express your grief—and your anger, too. Share them with Jesus. We have found that tears usually accompany healing; it is good if you are able to cry, even sob. In our culture many of us learned that it is a weakness to cry, and, yet, Jesus wept openly when his friend Lazarus died (*Jn.* 11:36), and we need to be set free to cry. Somehow, crying in the presence of Jesus usually changes into deep peace in a few minutes' time. The mother who has miscarried may have borne her pain alone and saved up many tears that need to be expressed in order to lift her depression. At times Jesus actually seems to hold the mother in his arms, as an older brother would, while she weeps. As Psalm 56 says: "You have noted my agitation; now collect my tears in your wineskin!" (v. 8)

4) Then forgive your doctor, or your husband, or anyone else you may blame for contributing to the miscarriage. (Perhaps you need to forgive yourself.)

5) Next, in Christ's presence, ask forgiveness of your child (wherever he may now be in God's kingdom) if you feel guilty about anything you did that might have contributed to the miscarriage. For instance, you and your husband may have incessantly quarreled during the time of your pregnancy; or, in times of loneliness, you may have given way to depression or self-pity; or you may have neglected your health (for example, studies indicate that babies born to mothers who smoke are often significantly undersized).

6) Last, we ask the mother to imagine Jesus letting her hold her child. While she holds her child she can say all those things she wanted to say to her child but was never able. Again, amaz-

ingly, at this point, the Lord often lets her know the sex of her lost baby.[9]

We have already mentioned that the mother needs to deal with the grief over the loss of her miscarried baby if she is going to bond well with the next child she conceives. Often the mother holds on to her grief and cherishes it ("shadow grief" it is called) because grieving is the one way she knows of keeping alive the memory of her lost child. There is no funeral, no tombstone and everyone else, including her husband, will probably forget about the baby she once carried so close to her heart. Only when she really *knows* that her child is with God and that she will see him once again will she be free to let go of her grief and depression.

If she becomes pregnant soon after the miscarriage in an attempt to make up for her loss, she may have a hard time loving and bonding with her next child; grieving and bonding cannot easily be carried on at the same time. She may also be unduly afraid of losing this next child—a fear that may be communicated to the fetus. All of this makes it imperative that we learn to pray for parents—especially mothers—who have lost their unborn babies!

ABORTION

St. Augustine said that, while we *hate* sin, we must *love* the sinner. In the human order this is almost impossible; it takes God's gift to combine a real hatred of sin and love for the sinner. When we love a person who has sinned we tend to condone his or her sin—in this case abortion. On the other hand, an active crusader against abortion may lack compassion toward women who obtain abortions. (A group of women who are deeply compassionate is WEBA—Women Exploited By Abortion, who offer alternatives to help pregnant women who are being pressured into having an abortion. Almost all of the regional officers of WEBA have themselves suffered an abortion.)

With nearly 1.5 million abortions being performed every year in the United States, there are many women—men, of course, are also responsible—who bear the suffering of having made such a decision to end the life they bore within them. Some women seem convinced that they did the right thing in having an abortion, but others come to experience guilt afterward—or even during the abortion procedure itself. According to one counselor, some 25 percent of her clients who relive their experience start to shake and cry out, as they relive the death agony of their child. This indicates that, even at the time, many mothers realize that what they are doing is wrong. The hurt of abortion, however, is so deep and poignant that it is often repressed, and the woman will seldom reveal her pain to anyone outside a deep relationship of trust.

Our friend Dr. Susan Stanford has written a powerful book on her own abortion experience and subsequent healing, in which she relates her own feelings of guilt and emptiness following "the procedure":

"In the next hour and a half my body slowly recovered from the pain and shock of the suction machine. Not so my psyche. The counselor, Julie, had warned me that I might experience a sense of loss. But this was emptiness. Desolation. Or something worse that can never be named. Once I had had a personality, a life, a soul. Now I was a body with broken pieces inside. It was that sense of shattering that I could not get a grip on. . . .

"After another hour the nurse returned to check on me. She said I could get up and go home. . . . Dressing, I felt as if I were clothing a plaster mannequin. The arms did not belong to me but to a stranger.

"When I walked to the outer room of the clinic I had to pass

Julie's office. She glanced up from a stack of paperwork. 'How are you doing?'

"I nodded and kept on walking.

"I don't know what would have come out of me if I'd opened my mouth. There was too little left of the real me to speak."[10]

After describing her own personal feelings of desolation, Dr. Stanford generalizes about her observations as a professional counselor:

> One of the most universal aftereffects of abortion is the feeling of guilt and loss. In my own practice some post-abortion women may initially deny feeling guilty and consequently avoid the topic of their abortions early on in the counseling relationship. However, invariably the topic comes up, perhaps around the anniversary due date or death date. When I've asked my clients how they feel about it in retrospect more than 90 percent share they feel some level of guilt feelings. Other women, who perhaps have to come to counseling with the presenting problem being the aftereffects of their abortion, define their feelings ranging from a pervasive dullness or depression to overpowering remorse and regret.[11]

During the time Judith worked as a psychologist in a psychiatric unit in Boston, she observed a remarkable phenomenon (noted by various other psychologists, and written up in several studies)—that some patients would become suicidal at certain times of the year. Their suicidal tendencies were so regular and predictable that their families would check them into the hospital for, say, the month of November. The staff found, on checking their family history with the patient's mothers, that these mothers had attempted an abortion in that particular time frame (e.g., November) when they were carrying that little unborn child. Somehow, the mother's desires had become imprinted upon her unborn baby so that even now the adult patient, many years later, was dedicated to carrying out his or her mothers' wishes. Usually the mother had never told her children that she had tried an abortion. And yet, somehow, the child knew! The link between mother and child is far stronger than most of us suspect.

Another amazing element in this pattern is that the patient usually attempts (or contemplates) suicide using a method similar to the one the mother had planned on using. If, for example, the mother had attempted an abortion by taking some drug, her child—now adult—will attempt to end it all by taking an overdose of drugs.

HOW TO PRAY

If you have had an abortion, and have later come to regret your earlier decision, here are some of the steps in prayer that you can take. (The same would be true of a man who pressured a woman into having an abortion. Some psychologists say that an abortion affects the man as deeply as it does the woman, but that he usually won't talk about it or seek help.)

1) *REPENT.* Tell God that you are sorry for what you have done. A Catholic would confess the sin in the presence of a priest, but it is good for anyone to confess to a minister or another Christian; "So confess your sins to one another, and pray for one another, and this will cure you" *(Jm.* 5:16). When we speak our sins out to a trusted person—ideally a minister—we bring these sins out from the darkness into the light and there, in the light, Jesus will forgive and heal us.

The person who has heard your confession of repentance,

can then ask Jesus Christ to forgive you or can proclaim that you are forgiven and that God has set you free.

After you have confessed, you may feel a great weight lift off your shoulders—and you may sense an experience of lightness, as well. The liberating Word of God has set you free.

But we must also be honest and state that some people still *feel* a lingering guilt, even though they *know* in faith that the Lord has forgiven them. They know that they caused a little unborn child to die; nothing can ever change that. That child will never walk in the sunlight; will never grow on this beautiful earth. "If I caused someone to die, I don't have the right to live," such a person might think. The woman (or man) may not be able to *forgive herself!* This felt guilt that lingers on in the emotions can be healed in the following steps.

2) *ASK YOUR CHILD TO FORGIVE YOU.* Anytime we have unjustly injured someone, we need to ask forgiveness. That little baby that was aborted is still alive—somewhere in God's kingdom, in the Communion of Saints. So you need to ask his or her forgiveness for the injury you have done. Jesus can bring your plea for forgiveness to that little child.

I remember one time when a young woman and her boyfriend came to me two years after they had gotten an abortion. The man had pressured his girlfriend into having the abortion, because they were not married. They were no longer seeing each other, but had—separately—come to realize the wrong they had done. So they came together to the prayer room at Merton House in St. Louis to bring their guilt and pain before the Lord.

The first thing I asked them to do was to confess their sin to God (as they had to me) and ask for his forgiveness. After they had done this, I proclaimed to them Jesus' forgiveness for their sin. Next, I suggested that she ask her child (in the Spirit, as it were) to forgive her for ending its life. She had a hard time saying it out loud but she was able, closing her eyes, to ask forgiveness of her child, wherever it was in God's kingdom, in the Communion of Saints.[12] Quietly, but with real feeling, she asked her baby's pardon.

Then I began to pray for her, and, as I prayed, she gently rested, with a beautiful smile on her face. After resting for about five minutes she sat up and shared what had happened.

In a vision she had seen God the Father; who was holding in his arms a two-year-old boy[13]—just the age her child would have been if he had lived in this world. What really impressed her was that her baby and God the Father[14] were both totally happy. God was rocking her little boy (she could see her child was a boy), who was laughing.

At this point, most of her fear was healed: she now *knew* that her baby was happy and was with God.

Next, God the Father turned toward her with a most beautiful smile, and she knew, deep in her heart, that he had forgiven her, too.

When the two left the prayer room, after only an hour of counsel and prayer, they were changed—especially the woman. Guilt and shame were lifted from their hearts and, in their place, God had given them new life, forgiveness and joy.

3) *FORGIVE THOSE WHO HAD ANYTHING TO DO WITH THE ABORTION.* You also may need to forgive anyone who pressured you into having the abortion: your parents, for instance, or your boyfriend. And, you may also need to forgive your counselor, or the doctor and nurses, into whose power you committed yourself and your child's destiny.

4) If you are from a sacramental church, you would do well to *HAVE A SERVICE CONDUCTED* for your dead child.

Some Christians do not, in good faith, believe in praying for the dead. For them, the service would be a memorial service—a final closure on the death of the little one, a formal saying goodbye, that leave-taking we all need when someone we know and love dies.

St. Paul recognizes a similar custom (without necessarily approving it) among the Corinthians:

> If this were not true, what do people hope to
> gain by being baptized for the dead? If the dead
> are not ever going to be raised, why be baptized
> on their behalf? *(1 Co.* 15:29).

For Catholics and other Christians who believe in praying for the dead, it would be beautiful to have a Mass of the Resurrection celebrated for the happiness of the little infant. This prayer experience will be specially powerful if you personally know the priest who will celebrate the Mass. Chances are, with an abortion, that the group that comes together will be small, which gives you a good chance to voice your own personal prayers.

What good news it is for us to know that if we have experienced the sadness of accidentally losing a child through miscarriage, or have purposely done so through abortion, the love of Jesus can restore us through healing and forgiveness.

> But the souls of the virtuous are in the hands of God,
> no torment shall ever touch them.
> In the eyes of the unwise, they did appear to die,
> their going looked like disaster,
> their leaving us, like annihilation;
> but they are in peace *(Ws.* 3:1–3).

Appendix Two

STAGES OF DEVELOPMENT:
WHAT TO PRAY FOR

(*by Francis*)

When Judith was pregnant we wanted to know, like most parents, how our unborn child was developing. So, we went to the library and took out books with illustrations showing the fetus at each stage of its development.[1] This helped us to picture our child, developing in secret, and it also helped to give us some sense of how to pray as the months went by.

So, we thought that the following summary of the fetus's development might help you focus your thoughts as you pray, day by day, for your growing baby. (As you know, the size of unborn children varies widely, so the sizes and weights given here are only approximate.)

At the end of the
FIRST MONTH
    SIZE 1/4 inch
    DEVELOPMENT
      Already your child's *heart* has started to beat. (It began beating somewhere around the twenty-fourth day after conception, although, as yet, it has only a single chamber.)

A very simple *spinal cord,* a groove that will close over at four weeks, has started to form.

At four weeks the *eyes* and *ears* are beginning to show.

Your child is growing about 1/25 of an inch every day.

SCRIPTURE

If I say, "Surely the darkness will hide me
    and the light become night around me,"
even the darkness will not be dark to you;
    the night will shine like the day,
    for darkness is as light to you.
For you created my inmost being;
    you knit me together in my mother's womb.
I praise you because I am fearfully and wonderfully made;
    your works are wonderful,
    I know that full well *(Ps.* 139:11–14, NIV).

At the end of the
SECOND MONTH
SIZE 1 1/8 inch

DEVELOPMENT

Your child's tiny *face* and its features are now forming.

The head and neck comprise one half the length of your baby's body (by comparison a newborn's head is one quarter of its body length).

Your child is no longer technically an embryo, but is now a fetus. Everything that is to be found in a fully developed human being is now being established.

The *muscles* are starting to move and exercise, but the heart has already been beating for a month.

The little *limbs* are starting to differentiate. The fingers are faintly visible, although the foot still looks like a paddle (because the hands develop faster than the feet).

The *internal organs* are starting to develop. As his mus-

cles develop, your baby can express his likes and dislikes by
kicking and jerking (Week 8), although you may not be able
to feel these movements as yet.

SCRIPTURE

> My frame was not hidden from you
>> when I was made in the secret place.
> When I was woven together
>> in the depths of the earth,
>> your eyes saw my unformed body.
> All the days ordained for me
>> were written in your book
>> before one of them came to be.
> How precious to me are your thoughts, O God:
>> How vast is the sum of them!
> Were I to count them,
>> they would outnumber the grains of sand.
> When I awake,
>> I am still with you *(Ps.* 139:15–18, NIV).

At the end of the
THIRD MONTH

> *SIZE* 3 inches
>   1 ounce

> *DEVELOPMENT*

> Your child's *arms, hands* and *fingers—legs, feet* and *toes*
> —are now fully formed. The nails are beginning to form.

> The external *ears* are now present.

> Although the lids are still fused, the *eyes* are developing
> fully, and the face is beginning to look human. The lips
> open and close.

> Your doctor may now be able to pick up a faint heartbeat.
> Blood cells are being produced by the liver and spleen.

> *SCRIPTURE*

> Can a woman forget her baby at the breast,

feel no pity for the child she has borne?
Even if she were to forget,
I shall not forget you.
Look, I have engraved you on the palms of my
hands . . .

(Is. 49:15–16, NJB).

At the end of the
FOURTH MONTH
   SIZE 7 inches
     4 ounces
   DEVELOPMENT
   Your baby now has a *distinct heartbeat.*
   The gristle is changing to *bone,* and most of the bones are now distinct in shape. The ribs are clearly visible.
   The eyes, ears and nose are continuing to take on a more human appearance. The eyebrows now take shape. Your baby can frown, squint and grimace. The eyes are sensitive to light but can see nothing distinctly.
   SCRIPTURE
   Thus says Yahweh who made you,
   who formed you in the womb; he will help you.
   Do not be afraid, Jacob my servant . . .
   For I shall pour out water on the thirsty soil
   and streams on the dry ground.
   I shall pour out my spirit on your descendants,
   my blessing on your offspring,
   and they will spring up among the grass,
   like willows on the bank of a stream *(Is.* 44:2–4, NJB).

At the end of the
FIFTH MONTH

SIZE 10–12 inches
        1/2–1 pound

DEVELOPMENT

Notice how fast your baby's *body* is growing! The top of your uterus now reaches to your navel. During this month, your baby will grow from about 6 inches long to 10 inches or more.

About this time the mother should be feeling her baby's first faint *kicks*.

The *eyes* are still closed, like a newborn kitten's. (The eyelids grow together at the beginning of the third month and open again in the seventh.)

Hair is beginning to appear—very short and "trimmed." Sometimes the thumb will slip into the mouth—preparing for sucking.

The *ears* are nearly complete and your baby is now hearing. It is no longer a silent world for your baby, who can probably hear your voice, but especially your heart and the sounds you make eating and drinking. From outside he can hear Daddy's voice, the radio, TV, traffic and music. So, if you aren't already talking to your baby, now is a good time for you and Daddy to start. On the other hand, you should protect your baby, as much as possible, from sudden, violent noise.

SCRIPTURE

I lift up my eyes to the mountains;
     where is my help to come from?
My help comes from Yahweh
     who made heaven and earth.
May he save your foot from stumbling;
     may he be your guardian, not fall asleep!

You see—he neither sleeps nor slumbers,
  the guardian of Israel.
Yahweh is your guardian, your shade,
  Yahweh, at your right hand.
By day the sun will not strike you,
  nor the moon by night.
Yahweh guards you from all harm
  Yahweh guards your life,
Yahweh guards your comings and goings,
  henceforth and forever *(Ps.* 121:all, NJB).

At the end of the
  SIXTH MONTH
    SIZE 11–14 inches
        1 pound or more
    DEVELOPMENT
    Your baby's *eyelashes* are forming. The *fingernails* extend now to the ends of the fingers. Your baby *hears clearly* and may move its body to the rhythm of your speech. It listens all the time now. The rudiments of language are laid down in the womb[2], and your baby can respond to music. Studies indicate that babies relax while listening to Mozart and Vivaldi (if you like classical music), but tense up when Beethoven and Brahms are played[3]. (This surprised me, too!) They also react against rock music. How wonderful it would be if you (and your husband) would sing to your child! Even before birth you and your husband can bond with your baby, who will recognize your voices later, after birth. (Recall, too, the examples we gave earlier of people who were able to remember music they heard in utero.) (It may be comforting for you to know that some babies born this early can survive.)
    SCRIPTURE
    . . . The angel answered . . . "Your cousin Elizabeth

also, in her old age, has conceived a son, and she whom people called barren is now in her sixth month, for nothing is impossible to God." Mary said, "You see before you the Lord's servant, let it happen to me as you have said." And the angel left her.

Mary set out at that time and went as quickly as she could into the hill country to a town in Judah. She went into Zechariah's house and greeted Elizabeth. Now it happened that as soon as Elizabeth heard Mary's greeting, the child leapt in her womb and Elizabeth was filled with the Holy Spirit. She gave a loud cry and said, "Of all women you are the most blessed, and blessed is the fruit of your womb. Why should I be honored with a visit from the mother of my Lord? Look, the moment your greeting reached my ears, the child in my womb leapt for joy" *(Lk.* 1:36–44, NJB).

At the end of the
SEVENTH MONTH
> *SIZE* 14–17 inches
> 2–3 pounds
> *DEVELOPMENT*

There is now a special reason to thank God, because your baby, if born this month, has a good chance of surviving. The eyelids are now separating and the eyes open. These last three months of pregnancy are especially important for intrauterine bonding. The fetus may be able *to feel the mother's emotions,* as well as to sense them, so the mother's attitudes toward her baby and toward life become increasingly crucial. Her religious faith will prove especially life-giving at this stage. On the other hand, the shock of parents fighting may be picked up by the fetus, just as their love and a peaceful, supportive relationship can help provide a spiritual, emotional security for their unborn child. Within a fraction of a second of the mother's experiencing strong fear, the baby's heart starts pounding twice as fast. If the mother is occasionally fearful and angry, this will help her unborn child, but if she is angry, bitter or fearful over a prolonged period, then it will prove harmful. So, take whatever steps you need to provide as loving and peaceful an environment as you can for yourself—and, in consequence —for your child.

If something should happen over which you have little control—for instance, if there is a tragedy in your family or if you find you are basically unhappy about leaving your job —then ask for prayer, to free you in relation to these events and to moderate your emotional response to them.

Sometime between the sixth and eighth months your baby will develop the ability to *remember* experiences.

Your child's *sleeping patterns* after birth will be influenced by your own sleeping patterns at present.

SCRIPTURE

How blessed are all who fear Yahweh,
    who walk in his ways!
Your own labors will yield you a living,
    happy and prosperous will you be.
Your wife a fruitful vine
    in the inner places of your house.
Your children round your table
    like shoots of an olive tree.
Such are the blessings that fall
    on those who fear Yahweh.
May Yahweh bless you from Zion!
May you see Jerusalem prosper
    all the days of your life,
and live to see your children's children!
                    (Ps. 128:1–5, NJB).

At the end of the
EIGHTH MONTH
SIZE 16–18 inches
     4–5 pounds
DEVELOPMENT

During this month your baby will grow another two pounds or more. If born now it will have a *very good* chance of survival. By the thirty-second week the neural circuits in your baby's brain will be as advanced as a newborn's. Therefore, your baby has a good deal of conscious awareness. The sleeping and waking states are now distinct.

SCRIPTURE

Always be joyful, then, in the Lord; I repeat, be joyful. Let your good sense be obvious to everybody. The Lord is near. Never worry about anything; but tell God all your desires of every kind in prayer and petition shot through with gratitude, and the peace of God which is beyond our understanding will guard your hearts and your thoughts in Christ Jesus. Finally . . . let your minds be filled with everything that is true, everything that is honorable, everything that is upright and pure, everything that we love and admire—with whatever is good and praiseworthy *(Ph.* 4:4–8, NJB).

At the end of the
NINTH MONTH
SIZE at birth: 20 inches, on the average
                7 pounds, on the average
DEVELOPMENT

In this, the last month, all your baby's systems are simply continuing to grow to the point where he can survive and thrive at birth. Now is a good time to pray—without anxiety—that everything goes well in the actual birth process. If you are going to give birth using a natural method, practice with your husband (or partner) until the process—the breathing and all—becomes second nature. Above all, ask Jesus to fill you with great joy and anticipation of all that is about to take place!

SCRIPTURE

At this time the disciples came to Jesus and said, "Who is the greatest in the kingdom of Heaven?" So he called a little child to him whom he set among them. Then he said, "In truth I tell you, unless you change and become like little children you will never enter the kingdom of Heaven. And so, the one who makes himself as little as this child is the greatest in the kingdom of Heaven. Anyone who welcomes one little child like this in my name welcomes me" *(Mt.* 18:1–5, NJB).

A woman in childbirth suffers, because her time has come; but when she has given birth to the child she forgets the suffering in her joy that a human being has been born into the world. So it is with you: you are sad now, but I shall see you again, and your hearts will be full of joy, and that joy no one shall take from you *(Jn.* 16:21–22, NJB).

NOTES

INTRODUCTION

1. Francis MacNutt, *The Prayer That Heals* (Ave Maria Press; Notre Dame, Ind., 1981).

2. Dr. Thomas Verny, *The Secret Life of the Unborn Child* (Summit Books; New York, 1981). If you are interested in the influences that determine an unborn child's psychological health, we highly recommend this eminently readable book.

3. Ibid., p. 50.

CHAPTER ONE

1. "Have you not read that the creator from the beginning 'made them male and female' and that he said: 'This is why a man must leave father and mother, and cling to his wife, and the two become one body'? They are no longer two, therefore, but one body" *(Mt.* 19:4–6).

2. Francis MacNutt, *The Prayer that Heals* Ave Maria Press; Notre Dame, Ind., 1981).

3. Dr. Conrad Baars, *Feeling and Healing Your Emotions* (Bridge Publishing Co.; Plainfield, N.J., 1979), pp. 82–84.

4. Francis MacNutt, *The Power to Heal* (Ave Maria Press; Notre Dame, Ind., 1977). Chapter 2 discusses this subject of healing through touch at some length.

5. We used Barclay's commentaries, such as *The Gospel of Matthew,* Vols. I and II, by William Barclay (Westminster Press; Philadelphia, Pa.,

1975). While Barclay lacks some understanding of the charismatic dimension of the spiritual gifts, his writing is eminently helpful and readable.

6. A fine book, with photographs, that can help you follow your child's development is *A Child is Born* by Lennart Nilsson (Delacorte Press; Garden City, N.Y., 1977). To help you in this we have added an Appendix to this book entitled "Stages of Development."

7. Primitive science taught that the male seed somehow congealed the mother's blood to form an embryo.

8. Francis MacNutt, "Prayers for the Unborn Child," *Charisma* magazine, Nov. 1983, pp. 24–32.

CHAPTER TWO

1. Frederick Leboyer, *Birth Without Violence* (Knopf; New York, 1975).

2. My dad had cancer of the bladder. At the time this chapter was first written (two years ago), the medical treatment did not seem to be helping and we were really worried. That, of course, is why we asked our friends to pray. Then in July 1985, while we were speaking at a conference in Los Angeles, we received bad news: the chemotherapy treatment that he was receiving had not helped; the tumors were still there and his doctor was going to do a further biopsy and then take out the tumors—there were three of them—possibly even take out the bladder. Then, at a distance (my dad lives in Jackson, Kentucky), we got all our friends to storm heaven with prayer. What happened next was encouraging: the biopsy showed the tumors to be benign, even though they had seemed to be malignant. Then we flew to Kentucky to pray with my dad in person; we had three sessions of prayer with him (which included prayer for repentance and for his accepting Jesus into his life). On my dad's next visit to the hospital, the doctor found, to our delight, that the tumors had disappeared—*without any further medical treatment.* At the time of this writing, a year later, there has been no further evidence of cancer.

CHAPTER THREE

1. J. P. Migne, ed., *Epistles* 11.64 *Patrologia Latina*, (Paris, 1844–65), quoted by John Noonan in *Contraception* (Mentor Omega; New York,

1967), p. 188. Historically, *mandatory* celibacy for priests in the Roman Catholic Church goes back to the kind of attitude expressed by St. Gregory.

2. In this regard the polling firm of Yankelovich, Skelly & White just published a survey *(Woman's Day* magazine, June 1986) that indicates that only 55 percent of women in their first marriages believe that they got married for the right reasons; 41 percent said that they don't believe that they did. Furthermore, only half of these wives said that they would marry the same man again, while 38 percent said they wouldn't; the rest were undecided. When we consider that these are married women—not the ones who have already divorced—we realize how fractured most marriages in the United States are. This survey was published in the October and November issues of *New Woman* magazine.

3. The following is taken from a letter by a woman whose conception was a "mistake":

"When Francis was praying, the Lord called me to *feel* his presence with me all the way back to my conception. Because my parents had to get married, I had always felt as though I was an accident. Later, when at sixteen I became a Christian, I experienced real love for the first time in my life, and I felt God had a plan for my life that would involve full-time Christian work. But, instead, I simply moved from a very disturbed home into a Christian marriage that ended in abandonment and divorce.

"Last night, I experienced and felt at a deep level that *NO* part of my life has been an accident. *He* wanted *ME* to be born, and, in spite of all the circumstances of my life, *He has been there all the time.* All those things that I had viewed as accidents, he is working out for my good that I may be free to be the person he created me to be."

4. Frank Lake, *Tight Corners in Pastoral Counseling* (Darton, Longman & Todd; London, 1981), pp. 26–27.

5. "All that is good, all that is perfect, is given us from above; it comes down from the Father of all light" *(Jm.* 1:16, NJB).

CHAPTER FOUR

1. Dr. Frank Lake, *Tight Corners in Pastoral Counseling,* (Darton, Longman & Todd; London, 1981), pp. ix–x.

2. "Mary set out at that time and went as quickly as she could to a town in the hill country of Judah" *(Lk.* 1:39).

3. "Then God, who had specially chosen me while I was still in my mother's womb, called me . . . so that I might preach the Good News about him to the pagans" *(Ga.* 1:15).

4. Dr. Frank Lake, op. cit., p. 39.

5. Dr. Gerhard Rottman, "Untersuchungen über Einstellung zur Schwangerschaft und zur fotalen Entwicklung," *Geist und Psyche* (Kinder Verlag; Munchen, 1974), as quoted by Thomas Verny, *The Secret Life of the Unborn Child* (Summit Books; New York, 1981), pp. 48–49.

6. The new issue of surrogate mothers naturally makes us wonder what effect the surrogate pregnancy has upon the embryo. One surrogate mother was interviewed and gave her answer about her attitude toward the baby:

"People look at it like, 'How could I give away one of my kids?'

"Well, I couldn't give away one of my kids, either. But this wasn't my kid; it never was. From the very beginning, I made a promise with myself that this was not going to be a relationship."

From "Surrogates Are Really No Special Breed" by Janice Martin, St. Petersburg *Times,* Feb. 16, 1987.

7. Dr. Monika Tukesch, "Psychologie Faktoren der Schwangerschaft," dissertation, University of Salzburg, 1975. This dissertation was based on a study of two thousand women through pregnancy and birth. Summarized in Verny, *The Secret Life,* p. 47.

8. Verny, *The Secret Life,* p. 49, summarizing Dr. Dennis Stott, "Children in the Womb: The Effects of Stress," *New Society,* May 19, 1977, pp. 329–31.

9. Francis MacNutt's *The Prayer That Heals* (Ave Maria Press; Notre Dame, Ind., 1981) is an easy-to-read book that shows couples how they can pray together for healing.

10. Lake, op. cit., p. 16.

11. Ibid., p. 32.

12. This, of course, does not imply that all, or even most, eczema is caused by prenatal distress.

13. Lake, op. cit., p. 33. The other information in this paragraph is a summary of pp. 14–15 and 30–34.

14. Agnes Sanford, *The Healing Gifts of the Spirit* (Jove Books; New York, 1982), p. 20.

15. Occasionally, deliverance from a demonic force of rejection is also needed in this kind of prayer.

16. Among many worthwhile books on this subject we would recommend *Praying with Another for Healing* by Dennis and Matthew Linn, S. J., and Sheila Fabricant (Paulist Press; Ramsey, N.J., 1984); *Healing the Hidden Self* by Barbara Shlemon (Ave Maria Press; Notre Dame, Ind., 1982); *Healing Gifts of the Spirit* by Agnes Sanford (Jove Books; New York, 1982); *Transformation of the Inner Man* by John and Paula Sandford (Bridge Publishing; South Plainfield, N.J., 1982); *Emotionally Free* by Rita Bennett (Fleming Revell Co.; Old Tappan, N.J., 1982); and *Healing for Damaged Emotions* by David Seamands (Victor Books; Wheaton, Il., 1981).

17. This phenomenon of resting in the Spirit happens frequently in healing services. My understanding of it is contained in Chapter 15 of my book *The Power to Heal* (Ave Maria Press; Notre Dame, Ind., 1977).

CHAPTER FIVE

1. For information on how to pray about deliverance, I would recommend Don Basham's *Deliver Us from Evil* (Zondervan; Grand Rapids, Mich., 1972).

2. Derek Prince has an interesting cassette book (three cassette tapes), entitled *Curses: Cause and Cure*. (This book can be obtained through writing P.O. Box 300, Dept. 6, Fort Lauderdale, Fla. 33302.)

In this book, he lists six conditions that affect *entire* families that may *possibly* indicate the existence of some curse:

1. Repeated mental and emotional breakdowns.
2. Repeated or chronic sickness (especially when there is no clear medical diagnosis).
3. Repeated miscarriages or related female problems.
4. A record of marriage breakdowns and family strife.

5. Continuing financial insufficiency, especially when the income seems sufficient.

6. The person or family is accident prone.

Any or all of these conditions can, of course, result from other than spiritual factors and they should only be taken as indicators that there *may* be a curse upon the family.

3. We realize that some of our readers may be skeptical about the reality of the power of curses. Since it is beyond the scope of this book to show the need to be free some families from demonic influences and curses through prayer, we simply state our belief (backed up by experience) that such a need does exist. The long tradition of Christianity has understood the need for the power of the Spirit to set people free from bondage to evil. I used to think it strange that in the traditional rite of Roman Catholic baptism there was an exorcism prayer for the infant. How in the world could I be praying such a prayer for an innocent child? But I now understand a little of the reason for such a precautionary exorcism. *Skepticism* about a *common* need for us to be freed from the influence of the demonic realm is a recent historical development. One book that may be a help in this is *Deliverance Prayer,* edited by M. and D. Linn, S.J., (Paulist Press, Ramsey, N.J., 1980).

CHAPTER SIX

1. Dr. Thomas Verny, *The Secret Life of the Unborn Child* (Summit Books; New York, 1981), pp. 46, 50.

2. Ibid., pp. 45–46.

3. Agnes Sanford, *Healing Gifts of the Spirit* Jove Books; New York, 1982). We recommend this book, in particular, for any depressed person seeking healing through prayer.

4. Verny, op. cit., p. 65.

5. Ibid., p. 57

6. Frank Lake, *Tight Corners in Pastoral Counseling* (Darton, Longman & Todd; London, 1981), p. 40–41

7. Ibid., p. 41.

8. Verny, op. cit., p. 70

9. Among books that help us learn how to pray for healing for one another we recommend, *The Prayer that Heals* by Francis MacNutt (Ave Maria Press, 1981); *Healing Life's Hurts* by Matthew and Dennis Linn, S.J. (Paulist Press; New York, 1978), a step-by-step approach to inner healing; and *Healing the Greatest Hurt* by Dennis and Matthew Linn and Sheila Fabricant (Paulist Press; New York, 1985), which deals with healing the depression and stress caused by *death.*

CHAPTER SEVEN

1. Joan Lunden, "Connecting Early," *Health,* March 1985.

2. Lisa Levitt Ryckman, "Doctor Believes Bringing Up Baby Should Start Before Birth," *Macon Telegraph and News,* Feb. 26, 1986.

3. Ibid.

4. F. Rene Van de Carr, "Perinatal Psychology: Birth of a Field," *Brain/Mind Bulletin,* Sept. 30, 1985.

5. John Grossman, "The Ultimate Nursery School?" *Health Magazine,* March 1985.

6. Thomas Verny, *The Secret Life of the Unborn Child* (Summit Books; New York, 1981), p. 41.

7. Ibid., p. 40.

8. Charles Spezzano, "Prenatal Psychology: Pregnant With Questions," *Psychology Today,* May 1981, p. 51.

9. Fraiberg, Selma, "How a Baby Learns to Love," reprint from *Redbook Magazine,* May 1971.

10. Ibid.

11. La Leche League, *The Womanly Art of Breastfeeding* (Interstate Printers and Publishers). This fine book can be ordered from La Leche League International, 9616 Minneapolis Ave., Franklin Park, Ill. 60131.

12. Ibid., p. 151.

CHAPTER EIGHT

1. Dr. Silvia Feldman, *Choices in Childbirth* (Grosset & Dunlap; New York, 1978), p. 8.

2. Dr. Thomas Verny, *The Secret Life of the Unborn Child* (Summit Books: New York, 1981), p. 71.

3. Ibid., p. 107.

4. Ibid., p. 98.

5. Ibid., p. 99.

6. Beth Ann Krier, "Can You Remember Your Birth?" St. Petersburg *Times*, March 20, 1981.

7. Verny, op. cit., p. 192.

8. David Cheek, "Pre-Birth Memories Appear to Have Lasting Effect," *Brain Mind Journal*, Vol. 7, No. 5, Feb. 15, 1982, p. 1.

9. Dr. Ashley Montagu, *Touching, the Human Significance of the Skin* (Columbia University Press; New York and London, 1971), p. 63.

10. Dr. Silvia Feldman, *Choices in Childbirth* (Grosset & Dunlap; New York, 1978), p. 2.

11. Dr. Frank Lake, *Tight Corners in Pastoral Counseling* (Darton, Longman & Todd; London, 1981), pp. 18–19.

12. Montagu, op. cit., p. 82.

13. Ibid., pp. 82–83.

CHAPTER NINE

1. Thomas Verny, *The Secret Life of the Unborn Child* (Summit Books; New York, 1981), pp. 30–31, 49, 57.

2. Jerrold Shapiro, "The Expectant Father," *Psychology Today*, Jan. 1987, pp. 36–42.

3. Ibid., p. 42.

4. There are many fine works on inner healing. Here, among others, are two we can recommend to illustrate how you might pray for one another (or, if necessary, for yourself alone):
    Healing the Hidden Self by Barbara Shlemon (Ave Maria Press; Notre Dame, Ind., 1982), and
    You Can Be Emotionally Free by Rita Bennett (Fleming Revell Co.; Old Tappan, N.J., 1982).

5. Several cassette tapes on this subject might be helpful here: *Our Perception of God* (#403) and *Healing Our Image of God* (#405) by

Judith MacNutt and *Healing Our Image of God* (#402) by Brennan Manning. These tapes are available through Christian Healing Ministries, 256 E. Church St., Jacksonville, Fla. 32202.

6. A good book describing how the husband's love helps the wife during pregnancy is *Husbands and Pregnancy* by William G. Genne (Association Press; New York, 1956).

CHAPTER TEN

1. I realize that many of our readers may not be familiar with prayer for deliverance from evil spirits. For those who would wish to investigate this topic further I recommend *Deliverance Prayer* (Paulist Press; New York, 1981), edited by Fathers Matthew and Dennis Linn, SJ, with chapters by a dozen authors (including myself), most of them Catholic priests.

2. Francis MacNutt, *The Power to Heal* (Ave Maria Press; Notre Dame, Ind., 1977). Chapter 15 describes what I have discovered about this phenomenon of "resting in the Spirit."

APPENDIX ONE

1. Thomas Verny, *The Secret Life of the Unborn Child* (Summit Books; New York, 1981) pp. 46–49.

2. Ibid., p. 89.

3. Ibid.

4. Ibid., pp. 87–88.

5. Seeing a marriage counselor can be a great help, especially if the counselor will pray for the couple.

6. "So then, if you are bringing your offering to the altar and there remember that your brother has something against you, leave your offering there before the altar, go and be reconciled with your brother first, and then come back and present your offering" *(Mt.* 5:23–24, NJB).

7. Harriet Schiff, *The Bereaved Parent* (Penguin; New York, 1977), p. 90.

8. Recently there have been criticisms of inner healing prayer. They are based on the supposition that people *demand* that Jesus do this or

that. In our prayers we do not demand anything of God. We *ask*. In faith we know that Jesus is already present. In his love and compassion he often seems to let people *know* that he is present and loves them. When *he chooses* to do this, it certainly helps in their healing!

9. Some Christians feel uncomfortable about praying in this way, although we see no particular difficulty with it. If you do not feel right about doing this, then simply *tell Jesus* what you would like to share with your child, who is somewhere in God's kingdom—in the Communion of Saints.

10. Dr. Susan Stanford, *Will I Cry Tomorrow? Healing the Post-Abortion Trauma*, (Fleming Revell; Old Tappan, N.J., 1987), pp. 72–73. We would strongly recommend that any woman who has had an abortion read this moving book. At the end there is an excellent section on how to pray for the healing of the abortion experience.

11. Ibid., p. 135.

12. This is a real, practical application of Christian belief in the Communion of Saints, which we proclaim each time we say the ancient Apostle's Creed.

13. Often when God helps people in this way, the mother becomes aware of the sex of her aborted child and sometimes of its name as well.

14. We know that God is spirit and is not like a human being; yet the Father often seems to appear to people in human form, the only reality that our humanity can relate to with feeling. Just as the Second Person of the Trinity becomes flesh as a human being, Jesus, so the Father occasionally appears to us in a way that we can relate to our littleness.

APPENDIX TWO

1. A complementary booklet called *Pregnancy in Anatomical Illustrations* is a fine brief summary of how the fetus develops. Carnation Healthcare Services (5045 Wilshire Blvd., Los Angeles, Calif. 90036) publishes it, and it can be found in many obstetricians' offices.

A more extended illustrated description of the fetus's development is contained in Lennart Nilsson's *A Child is Born* (Delacorte Press; New York, 1977).

2. Verny, Thomas, *The Secret Life of the Unborn Child* (Summit Books, New York, 1981), p. 33.

3. Ibid., pp. 21, 39.